THE BEST
FLY-FISHING TRIPS
MONEY CAN BUY

THE BEST
FLY-FISHING TRIPS
MONEY CAN BUY

PAT FORD

STACKPOLE
BOOKS

Copyright © 2006 by Stackpole Books

Published by
STACKPOLE BOOKS
5067 Ritter Road
Mechanicsburg, PA 17055
www.stackpolebooks.com

Printed in China

First edition

10 9 8 7 6 5 4 3 2 1

Photos by the author, except where noted.

Library of Congress Cataloging-in-Publication Data

The best fly-fishing trips money can buy / Pat Ford.
      p.   cm.
    ISBN-13: 978-0-8117-0179-2 (hardcover)
    ISBN-10: 0-8117-0179-4 (hardcover)
  1. Fly fishing.   I. Ford, Pat (T. Patrick)
SH456.B4393   2006
799.1'24—dc22
                                  2005037861

CONTENTS

FOREWORD

STU APTE

Many years ago, my mother was forced by the rigors of time to reside in an assisted-living facility in Miami. I remember one day when I was in a meeting with the administrator trying to discuss a number of her complaints and was pretty much being ignored. Finally, out of frustration I said, "Look, my attorney is Pat Ford. Since you don't seem to want to discuss this with me, you can talk to him." The administrator sat straight up and turned white. My mother received excellent care from that day on, but Pat refers to his role as a trial lawyer as his "day job." His real love is fly fishing and photography. I have known and fished with Pat for more than two decades, and within this book you will see why I am continually awed by his stills with a camera and gift for storytelling.

A short time after my wife, Jeannine, and I decided to have our wedding at Cheeca Lodge, we also decided who would be best to perform the ceremony. It was scheduled to be held on the beach, we had invited 168 of our friends, and we wanted a party that would top all previous parties in this part of the Florida Keys. After considerable thought and discussion, Jeannine and I asked Pat to perform the ceremony. He agreed, and to my chagrin told everyone he met over the next two months that he was "marrying Stu Apte in May." His rather dry sense of humor resulted in a lot of strange looks until the details were explained. The reason that I mention this sidebar is twofold. First, I want you to understand the type of relationship I have with Pat, and second, I wanted to be able to tell you that during this hour-long wedding ceremony, Pat had 170 people in the palm of his hand—he had them laughing, sometimes crying, sometimes applauding, and yes, sometimes cheering. This hopefully is what he is going to do to you as you go through the pages of this book, except for the crying part, that is.

Any endeavor to write about the best of anything is extremely difficult. To write a book about the best fly-fishing trips money can buy is an awesome undertaking, but it's designed to let you, the reader, share some of the joys and some of the frustrations in planning angling experiences in many of our favorite places around the world. As a Pan Am pilot for thirty-four years, a fishing guide, an angler, and at times, a photographer, I've fished for most of the species in most of the places that Pat describes so eloquently in photo and text within the pages of this book. I've sat down time after time when considering a new destination and wished that there was someplace I could go to find out what, where, when, and how to put the trip together. That's what Pat has done.

He tells you how to set up your trip, how to catch the fish once you get there, the best tackle to bring, and his photos literally take you there.

If you love to fly-fish and you're in the market for a great trip or a family vacation, you really need to read this book.

PREFACE

Of the few things that have stuck with me throughout my life, the most satisfying have been fly fishing and photography. I recall tying flies as a child growing up in northern New Jersey and, later on, financing my college years at Notre Dame through my sports photography. During my last year of Columbia Law School in 1968, the last six weeks of classes were cancelled by a series of protests over the Vietnam War. While everyone fretted about "rights," I spent most of my time fly-fishing in the reservoir streams an hour north of New York City. Probably the biggest break of my life came when the Navy JAG Corps sent me to Pensacola and then Key West instead of Vietnam, which allowed me to give in completely to the joy of saltwater fishing. I wrote my first article for *Salt Water Sportsman* magazine in 1969 and have managed to publish something somewhere almost every year since, just for the fun of it. Fortunately, my "day job" as a trial lawyer allowed me the opportunity to travel quite a bit and to fish for a variety of species of gamefish. After each expedition, I'd write an article for a magazine describing the trip—what went wrong, what went right, and what the fish were like. Eventually, my friends started telling me to put all these experiences along with my photos in a book to help others learn from what happened to me on my trips. So with the help of Stackpole Books—here it is.

I realize that there are a million excellent places and lodges that I haven't visited and lots of things I haven't done. What I tried to do is take a dozen or so of my favorite fishing trips and tell everyone else how to put that same trip together for themselves. At the end of each chapter, I've provided contact information for travel agents, outfitters, and guides that I can vouch for as reputable and knowledgeable. I'm confident that if they can't handle a request personally, they will be more than happy to direct you to someone who can. A lot of the chapters deal with the Florida Keys simply because of the magnificent variety of fishing that is available there. I haven't found anything that compares to South Florida. The fishing is fantastic year-round, and no matter what the weather, there is something to catch inshore or offshore somewhere. The flats from Miami to Key West have some of the best tarpon, bonefish, and permit fishing in the world. Key West is a light-tackle paradise in itself. Even when the wind is blowing 25 knots, you can still drift the flats and cast flies to sharks. There is always something going on, and you don't even have to leave the country.

The motivation behind this book was the difficulty I experienced in finding reliable information on when and how to fish particular locations. Whenever I would plan a trip, I'd try to learn as much about the area as possible, but that was easier said than done. What I always wanted to know was what weight rod did I need, what type of line, and what were the best flies to bring. For me, the anticipation and preparation are almost always as much fun as the trip itself. Usually I'd appear on a first-time trip with too much of the wrong stuff, but eventually I'd figure things out. I love to fly-fish, I love to travel to interesting places, and I love it when a plan comes together. There is nothing more satisfying than having a local guide ask to borrow some of your flies or notice that your rod and line combination is more effective than everyone else's. The flip side is getting to a place you've always wanted to fish and to find out that everything you'd been told was wrong. I've been in both of those situations, and if this book does nothing else, hopefully it will make a few angling vacations more fun for a few people.

ACKNOWLEDGMENTS

It may be a cliché by now, but lives are measured by the friends you make along the way, and the friends you make through fishing always seem to stick around through the rise and fall of the stock markets, divorces, hurricanes, accidents, and injuries, good times and bad. Perhaps it's because fishermen are such optimists—a truly great fish is always just around the next bend. Even when an angler has stood on the casting platform in 100-degree heat for hours without seeing a fish, he will suddenly jump down and change flies. Somehow, that totally irrational act will rejuvenate his hopes and allow him to stare at the water forever, knowing that that one perfect fish is just a few minutes away.

I could not have put this book together without the help of my friends. In fact, all of my friends and family made a contribution in one way or another, but several deserve to be thanked personally but not in any particular order.

Captain Bill Curtis went from an idol on *American Sportsman* to a friend that has fished with me for over thirty years. On his eightieth birthday, the Miami Beach Rod and Reel Club asked me to put on a roast for Bill. I considered it an honor, and I think he's still speaking to me.

Captain Rick Murphy did his very best to try to teach me how to catch tarpon, and now that he's a TV star and rated number 1 in the Redfish Tour, he still finds time to pole me around once in a while. Fortunately, I was not the one who put the fly through his ear.

Captain Eric Herstedt is younger than all of my children, but he is fast becoming a master at fly-fishing Florida Bay. In not too many years, he will take his place among the very best.

Chico Fernández was once described by Lefty Kreh as "the best fly caster I've ever seen." Chico provided my introduction to Judith Schnell at Stackpole Books and unselfishly offered to write the chapter on bonefish and permit. His photos are outstanding, and he is a pleasure to fish with even though he won't let me play my country music on the way down to Flamingo.

Stu Apte has been a friend for years and graciously offered to write an introduction in addition to putting his stamp of approval on the chapter texts. Stu never does anything fancy while he's fishing—he just puts the fly exactly where it has to be at just the right time. He makes everything look so easy.

Billy Pate has devoted most of his life to catching tarpon and billfish on fly. He pretty much founded the Golden Fly Invitation Tarpon Tournament and has allowed me to run it untethered for many years. Billy once caught a 173-pound tarpon while fishing alone. He managed to hook, fight, and gaff that fish without anyone else's help at age sixty. Not many people I know could do that at any age.

Captain Robert "RT" Trosset and I have fished together since he was impersonating a mechanic in Kings Point Marina in Key West in 1975. There's not much about Key West that he doesn't know, and he is a pleasure to fish with regardless of what time he gets to the dock in the morning. Captain Ted Lund has progressed from selling flies on Duval Street to the editor of *Fly Fishing in Salt Waters* magazine, and his help and photo contributions are greatly appreciated.

Andy Mill is probably the best tarpon fisherman on the planet these days, with the same style and talent that Stu Apte displayed in his youth. Andy dominates the Keys tarpon tournaments every spring, and his love of fly-fishing for tarpon is apparent in his chapter.

Bob Stearns has been around for decades, as both a fisherman and writer, and has helped me out in both areas on more occasions than I can remember.

Dr. Marty Arostegui has something like 140 International Game Fish Association (IGFA) world records to his credit and has caught fish on fly that many felt were impossible. He has thrown a fly at most everything that swims and truly deserved his Lifetime Achievement Award from the IGFA.

Neal Rogers has already published more books than I ever will, and his fishing and photography skills are outstanding. When Captain Tim Hoover refers to us as clones, I take it as a supreme compliment.

Dr. Al Forns has been the catalyst in my progression from film to digital photography, and his continuing help in developing my photography and computer skills is invaluable.

Mike Myatt and Rob Kramer at the IGFA have published my articles in their *Yearbook* for years and have encouraged me continually to keep writing and keep taking pictures of a sport we all truly love.

Tom Robinson, owner of the Rainbow King Lodge, introduced me to Alaska and a wilderness of beauty beyond compare. There is nothing like Alaska.

Alan Gadoury is the finest trout fisherman I have ever known. His expertise in Montana's spring creeks was enough to overcome my saltwater habits and is the only reason I ever caught anything out there.

Chuck Anceny owns a ranch in Big Sky with a spring-creek pond that is the most enjoyable place I have ever fished. The vacations I spent at Chuck's with my wife, Kay, and our dogs were the best. Chuck turned ninety-one in August 2005 and is an inspiration to everyone who knows him. He epitomizes everything that is strong and free about the West.

Lefty Kreh, Carl Hiaasen, Jeffrey Cardenas, Steve Yatomi, Larry Dahlberg, Rufus Wakeman, Steve and Randee Ward, Flip Pallot, Terry Gunn, Grant Cummings, Luis Gomez Jr., Jim Rist, Captains Randy Towe, Doug Kirkpatrick, Paul Tejera, Dave Denkert, Kris Suplee, Tim Hoover, and many others contributed to my projects in one way or another and all deserve my heartfelt thanks.

The photographs of me in the book were taken by the best photographers in the world—my friends.

Finally, and most of all, I have to thank my lovely wife, Kay, without whom my life clearly would have been unfulfilled and undoubtedly boring. Today she would rather stay home with her cavaliers, Dina and Henry, and paint than go fishing, but she is actually an excellent angler in her own right. During our years together, she has told me to do and not do a lot of things, but she has never told me that I couldn't go fishing. No one could ask for a better wife.

Bonefish and Permit

CHICO FERNÁNDEZ

The beauty of the flats in the Florida Keys is breathtaking.

The best you can get—a bonefish tailing over a sand bottom.

There are more huge bonefish in shallow water in South Florida and the Upper Florida Keys than any other place on the planet. And, if that's not enough, in the last ten years or so, the bonefish have been getting bigger and bigger. Where a big bonefish in the sixties and seventies in South Florida was usually around 12 pounds, today many bonefish are taken, on a fly rod, in the 13-, 14-, 15-pound range and bigger.

As a matter of fact, in the summer of 2005, Captain Dale Perez guided Chuck Sheeley of Columbus, Ohio, to an enormous bonefish while fishing in the Upper Keys right out of Islamorada. The monster measured $36\frac{1}{2}$ inches to the fork of the tail, which would put it around 38 inches overall. Since bonefish of 12 to 14 pounds typically measure 31 to 32 inches, you can only imagine how big this bonefish was. Mr. Sheeley decided to turn him back, so we'll never know, but most estimates of the weight of this fish are well over 17 pounds. Fortunately, he's still out there somewhere.

These trophy bonefish aren't easy. You will find that good casting skills and often a "brown trout" presentation are of the essence with a fly rod or any casting tackle, but they will take the right fly retrieved in a convincing manner. And when they do, you'll experience power from a fish shorter than 3 feet, as you never have before. . . . Interested?

You can have a very good day of bonefishing, or take a big double-figure bonefish, any day of the year in South Florida. But water temperature often dictates, more than

Tim Mahattey releases a gray ghost of the flats off Islamorada.

Going away tailing—a common sight but a hard cast.

any other factor, whether you'll see schools of bonefish or single large bones or whether you'll see them at all.

During warmer temperatures, you'll see tailing bonefish spread out over the flats, feeding in singles or pods of three or more fish. But when it gets real cold, they tend to leave the flats until it gets warm again. Even if you do see some fish cruising the flats during strong cold spells, they'll be moving slowly and not too anxious to feed.

So the time of year that you select to come to South Florida will dictate your chances of catching a bonefish, a real big bonefish, and whether or not the fish will be tailing. It will also dictate, within reason, your chances of having good weather.

In December, January, and February, the typical winter weather patterns will show repeated cold fronts with winds mostly from the north. In between these cold fronts, there are usually patches of warmer weather and calmer winds, generally from the east or southeast. It's right after these cold fronts, during the warming cycle, that fishing can be quite good, with bonefish becoming more active in the flats. And because they have been too cold to feed for a few days, they are more willing to take a fly. Pat Ford, for example, caught his largest bonefish, a 15-pounder, on bait on December 5 several years ago and then followed it up two weeks later with a 14-pounder on fly—both with Captain Rick Murphy in Biscayne Bay.

But in the Miami area and the adjacent outer Keys, sometimes one can see big schools of bonefish when the temperature is low, say in the 60s. Captain Chris Dean tells me that these schools can be very large, but the fish are in deeper water and moving slowly, and it may take a few good presentations to finally get one to strike.

Captain Tim Hoover holds up Neal Rogers's 15-pound bonefish. They don't get much bigger than this anywhere. LINDA ROGERS

Captain Rick Murphy with my largest bonefish on fly—close to 14 pounds.

The side of a bonefish is basically a mirror reflection of the bottom—look for the dark back to spot them.

Still, you must remember that as good an opportunity as the warm spells in the winter months can be, timing your trip between cold fronts is not always easy. It can be done if you can move fast when a friend or guide tells you it's warming, but it is always a gamble.

By March and April, the cold fronts appear less frequently, and you are not taking nearly as big a chance on the weather by booking a guide at this time of year. But it will be windy—very windy. March and especially April are the windiest months. However, it's worth it, because these are the months that produce the largest bonefish of the year, probably due to their spawning cycle. An added bonus at this time of year is that, with the relatively cooler water still in the flats, these big fish can produce spectacular long runs, especially when hooked on an oceanside flat.

By May, June, and even the first few days of July, the weather is warm enough for the bonefish's taste, but not too warm. There should be plenty of them feeding in the flats and often tailing. And because it's still not too hot, they should be on the flats all day long. Now you would think that with this great bonefishing going on there would be lots of anglers fishing for them at this time of year, but the fact is that there are only a few. You see, this is also the peak of tarpon season, and most fly fishers have "big silver" on their minds. So if you want bonefish in the spring, you'll find the shallow flats with little pressure, and the bonefish more than willing to take a well-presented shrimp or crab pattern.

As we get deeper into the summer, the middle of July, August, and September, we are now fishing in the hottest

An evening on the flats of Florida Bay is prime time for taking bonefish.

In summer, dawn on Biscayne Bay provides outstanding fishing for bonefish and permit.

time of the year. With air and water temperatures reaching the low 90s, it will probably be too hot in the flats for most bonefish during the middle of the day. This is the time to fish very early and late in the day. For the middle of the day, I recommend a big lunch and a long siesta. Indeed, many guides even offer a split fishing day in which they will take you out at dawn or nearly so, bring you back for that siesta we talked about, and then take you out again after four or five o'clock. This way you take advantage of the lower water temperatures, which will still be in the high 80s at best. And while a split trip may be more expensive sometimes, it's worth it, believe me.

Then by late September, October, and November, the water temperatures start to go down to a more civilized level, which is enough to make a difference to Mr. Bonefish. Now you'll see good bonefishing throughout the whole day, and there will still be plenty of tailers. This time of the year is also an excellent time to find the bigger bonefish in the flats up until the second or third strong cold front pushes through.

Eric Herstedt releases a fat permit off Elliott Key near Miami.

Often the first thing you spot is the black dorsal and tail of a permit.

Captain Bill Curtis's hands have released more Florida bonefish than any others on the planet, but the sun takes a toll.

Sometimes there is no substitute for the real thing, but we try anyway.

Besides all the big bonefish, South Florida has some of the largest permit you can ever find in the flats. So if you are interested, and you should be, make sure you carry a heavier rod rigged with a crab fly. When the tides get too deep for bonefish, the permit will start to show up.

Again, its possible to find permit in the flats year-round in South Florida and the Keys, but permit like even warmer temperatures than bonefish, so the time of year is very important. Winter months are usually not very good unless there is a serious warm spell. I would not book a trip in December, January, or February if your main target is permit.

In the Keys, March and April are usually very good months for fishing for permit. And by then, the cold fronts are less frequent and weaker, so water temperatures are up. March has been a traditionally great month for permit in Key West and Miami.

Also, the warmer months from July until the first cold front arrives in November will produce lots of permit in the flats on a strong incoming tide. You could find a big permit, say over 30 pounds, any time during these warm months anywhere from Miami to Key West.

Now for some fishing advice: The single most common complaint of a flats fishing guide is the casting ability of the angler. This has not changed since I started fly fishing back in the fifties. So please make it a point to practice, and if possible, take some casting lessons from a qualified instructor. You'll be glad you did, and so will your guide.

When casting to a bonefish or permit, remember that they are mostly feeding against the tide, so try casting just outside their area of awareness, which is usually a few feet in front of a moving fish, and a bit closer for a tailing fish. And be even more aggressive (meaning cast closer) when fishing permit. You need to practice shooting a fly 50 feet with no more than two backcasts. Speed is often just as important as accuracy.

Booking a guide. Select your guide from the recommendation of a fellow fly fisher who has fished the guide or from a tackle shop you trust. If you have more than a couple of days to fish, say four days or more, I would suggest that you split your fishing days between two different guides, just in case. You could end up with a guide that does not want to work (pole for you), or it may be that you two just don't have good chemistry. But by fishing two guides, you have a better chance of finding, for future trips, someone you enjoy spending the day with. And if it turns out you like both guides, great, you

RT Trosset poles while Steve Ward makes a cast on the gulfside flats north of Key West.

have two names to call, and you probably will learn lots of different fishing techniques from each of them. Trust me, this works.

I'd say that the best time to book a guide for the Upper Florida Keys or South Florida is right now. The best guides are often booked a year ahead of time, especially if you are thinking of the spring season. Many people book the same guide for the same days every year—if you're new to the scene, you need to find those few extra days he can squeeze you in. If you want to fish April through June, you'd better call in September.

Tackle. The combination of the heavier flies we use for these extra big bonefish and the often windy conditions dictates that you use a heavier outfit than you probably would in the Bahamas, Belize, or Yucatan. A 9-foot, 8- or 9-weight will handle any big bonefish fly in almost any condition, providing you've learned to cast these heavier rods.

Hiromi Kuboki ties the most fantastic crab flies I have ever seen.

Captain Bill Curtis at age eighty is still helping anglers like artist Jean Eastman catch their first bonefish on fly.

Captain Paul Tejera with a 15-pound "downtown Islamorada" bonefish. PAUL TEJERA

During calmer weather, smaller flies work better, and I'd take the 8, but on a windy day or when casting big heavy flies in 2 or 3 feet of water to mudding fish, you will want a 9. On flat, calm days with unweighted or lightly weighted flies, I've used a 7-weight with great success. Some anglers use a 10-weight rod for bones, but this is too heavy for my taste, even on windy days, and on calm days, you'll spook lots of fish with that heavy line. A 10-weight with a Merkin is perfect for permit, however.

When fishing permit, you have to cast a very chunky and heavy crab fly in most cases, and this requires a heavier fly line to carry and turn over the fly. My preference is a 9-foot, 10-weight outfit. Some anglers even use a 10-weight rod with an 11-weight line for permit. While the heavier 11 line will carry the big crabs just fine, the overall outfit is just too heavy for my taste. Again, the heavier line can spook fish on calm days, but permit fishing is best with some wind, so sometimes it doesn't matter. It's really a matter of personal taste.

For both the big bonefish and permit, any reel with 200 yards of backing and a good drag will do fine. I even fish them with a large clicker drag when I'm in the mood. The trick is in a good presentation, convincing retrieve, and clearing the line. After that, you're on your way.

The fly line you need for both bonefish and permit is a floating line that does not get too soft or limp in the extremely hot and humid tropical weather. Usually one with a stiff mono or braided mono core will shoot well through the guides instead of hanging on the guides like wet linguini. You'll find that most fly-line manufacturers make fly lines for tropical conditions with the above cores in a bonefish tarpon or even a permit taper.

On the average day, a 12-foot leader is my standard leader length, including a 30-inch tippet or so. On very windy days, I go down to 10 feet but not much shorter. And on calm days, I may go another foot or so longer than 12 feet. But if it's flat calm, instead of a super long leader, I'd rather go to a lighter outfit with the same 12-foot leader. Say from a 9- to an 8-weight, or from an 8 to a 7. It spooks less fish and is more fun to fish.

My standard tippet size for these big bones and the permit is usually 12-pound-test tippet. Occasionally for bonefish, I'll go down to a 10-pound test on very calm days and a 7-weight rod. Or I'll go up to a 16-pound test for permit on very windy days or when fishing close to lots of coral and sea fans. And I usually tie the fly with a loop (mostly a Duncan Loop) not just for better action, but because it sinks faster this way.

There are so many flies for bonefish in the Keys that one could write a book about them, literally. I would suggest you check in the local fly shops in the Keys and Miami for the best local patterns. But I'll tell you that I use more crab patterns on bones these days than any other and only crab patterns on permit. The Crab Critter in its many variations and the Merken are consistent producers. But there are a few shrimp patterns for bonefish that are killers too.

This permit fell for a Hiromi Crab.

On some days, the beauty of the place takes your breath away.

Captain Kris Suplee took a day off to catch this 29-pound permit on a fly off Marathon.

Captain Rick Murphy and Stu Apte show the rewards of wading the flats off Elliot Key.

Miscellaneous necessities. Bring a heavy Ziploc bag for your wallet and keys. If the car keys get wet, you may not be able to disconnect your alarm. And a wet billfold is no fun either.

Wear mostly long pants and long sleeves. If you go with shorts, be prepared to put on lots of sunscreen. A bandana, tied bandit style, will protect you not only from the sun, but also from windburn on your face during long runs. I use one often.

Bring shoes or sandals that are made specially for boating. Avoid those that leave dark marks on the boat deck. You'll get along with your guide much better this

There is no such thing as a small permit on fly.

The lips and mouth of a bonefish call for small flies.

way. You probably will not be doing much wading, but ask your guide just in case you need wading shoes.

Bring a hat or cap with a dark underbrim so there is little or no glare from it on your glasses.

High-quality polarized sunglasses are of the essence to see through the water. A warm color like amber or tan works best. Do not get grey or blue for the flats.

Good rain gear, with or without the pants, is also necessary, not only for rain, but also because it can get cold, especially during the late fall to spring or during a summer thunderstorm. Running back to the dock soaking wet is no fun.

In addition, a hook file, pliers, lens cleaner, fly-line dressing, and sunscreen should also be in your tackle bag.

Pat Dorsey's collection of Kwan flies.

Another visitor to Miami's flats.

Author Carl Hiaasen with a 14¹/₂-pound bonefish taken off Islamorada. Carl is as proficient with a fly rod as he is with a pen.

And talking about tackle bags, don't bring one that is too big. Remember that today's skiffs tend to be lighter and smaller, so they float higher and spook fewer fish with their bow wake. But that also means less hatch space. So a midsize tackle bag is all you need.

Also, I recommend you bring a camera (digital or film) to record that big bonefish and anything else exciting that may happen on the trip.

And finally, bring water, lots of water. And drink it throughout the day, even when you feel you are not thirsty. It can get real hot out there.

To book a day on the flats, call the Biscayne Fly Shop in Miami at (305) 669-5851, Florida Keys Outfitters in Islamorada at (305) 664-5423, or the Saltwater Angler in Key West at (305) 294-3248.

Good luck!

The single best spot for permit is the Marquesas Atoll west of Key West.

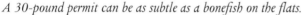

A 30-pound permit can be as subtle as a bonefish on the flats.

Tarpon

ANDY MILL

A perfect day on Biscayne Bay begins at dawn.

For ten years, my athletic roots took me to nose-bleed heights where I skied downhill at 80 mph in my quest to gain an Olympic medal. I was driven, passionate, and crazy until I broke my leg, my back, and my neck in the same year. Now, thirty years later, this all seems pale in comparison to how I feel about tarpon and the game we fly fishermen play to catch them. I have been running around the flats from Key West to Miami now for over fifteen years, and I have learned a lot about these wonderful fish—how to convince them to bite and how to fight them on a fly rod. Hopefully, my enthusiasm for this sport will become apparent in the following paragraphs and encourage you to spend a week in South Florida in the spring chasing *megalops atlantics*—a prehistoric dinosaur with fins, silver armor, and a bucket mouth with the texture of concrete.

Sometimes tarpon appear in the outskirts of the Everglades as early as December. These are big fish that move south fleeing the cold and sneak inshore when water temperatures rise above 74 degrees. It's not something you can plan on—when conditions are right, they just appear, hang out for a day or two, then disappear back into the Gulf. They provide a select group of guides and locals with spectacular fishing if they are very lucky. Some years, these "winter" tarpon never show up at all, but by mid-March or April, the waters of Florida Bay consistently

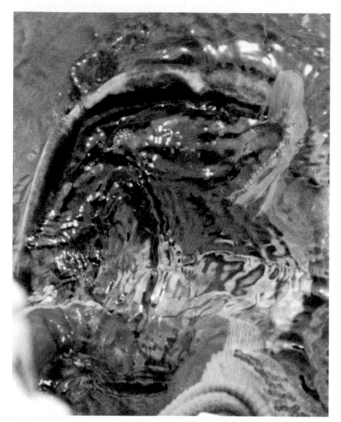

The mouth of a 130-pound tarpon is the size of a 5-gallon bucket with the texture of concrete.

In the winter, big tarpon can be found in Whitewater Bay whenever we have a few days of warm weather.

Captain Rick Murphy holds up a 140-pound tarpon for Dr. Linda Robinson, the only woman to win the Golden Fly Tarpon Tournament.

Landing a nice tarpon off Miami in June.

creep up over the 74-degree mark, and tarpon begin to appear in steady numbers.

The main problem with March in South Florida is the wind. Tarpon like nice, quiet mornings when the humidity has teardrops streaking down your car windows, and the flags are draped vertically down their poles. This is when the young cypress trees sprout their first green buds, and the big spring tides flood the flats. Tarpon need water temperature over 74 degrees to be even remotely happy, and clear, calm mornings, when a horizontal plane of water reaches out into the edge of the world, puts them into their comfort zone. Suddenly, they appear in channels, bights, and bays by the hundreds from Flamingo to Key West. Usually, they will stick around until a cold front pushes them back out to sea, which may be for a few days or a few weeks. In March, timing the weather is everything, but in April, migrating schools of tarpon will start swimming the shallow oceanside edges of the Florida Keys. For the next three months, through June and sometimes even July, the fish will swim back and forth between bridges and up and down the Atlantic coast from Miami to Key West.

Captain Tim Hoover releasing a toad-caught tarpon. The best place to hook a tarpon is right where this fly is.

Tarpon get into very shallow muddy water looking for mullet . . .

. . . and can be seen swimming around with their backs out of water.

One of the greatest aspects of fly fishing for tarpon is that they can be hunted in clear, shallow waters in sleek, quiet skiffs. This is team fishing, and you really need a guide if you hope to have any chance of success. Spring tarpon are migrating and are greatly affected by tides, wind, and moon phases. One day, a section of ocean will be alive with poons. A few days later, you might not see a fish. Every tarpon angler needs a guide who knows when and where to find the fish and who can pole him into position to make a 60-foot cast to a pod of silver kings that may be swimming in strings along the coast or laid up, motionless in the back country or Florida Bay. Flies that work on the Atlantic will get laughed at in the muddy water off Cape Florida. Casting and fly placement for a cruising fish is totally different from casting to a monster lying motionless over a grass bottom. Your guide will know when to fish which area, when the tides push the fish in tight to the banks, and when the tarpon will be floating at anchor in some remote corner of some remote bay. You can't fish for tarpon effectively without a guide. Even Stu Apte and Billy Pate hire a guide when they want to do some serious fishing. If you try to visit South Florida during the tarpon season and fish from your own boat unassisted, you will probably be very disappointed.

Alright, now let's assume you have booked a hotel in Islamorada and hired a guide for a week of tarpon fishing in May. The guide will get you to the right flats, will find you the fish, and, hopefully, put you into position for that perfect cast. At that point, it's all up to you, the angler. First, you need the right tackle and a quality pair of polarized glasses. You must have polarized sunglasses to see the

Big tarpon, lousy weather, good photo.

The power and violence of a tarpon's first few jumps is awesome.

fish, and don't ever let anyone tell you different. You also need a hat and more sunscreen than you can imagine.

The standard tarpon outfit is a 12-weight rod with a floating line. You need to be able to cast it accurately to 60 feet with one or two backcasts—yes, you need to practice if you live in Iowa. You will be wasting precious fishing time if you expect the guide to teach you how to cast an outfit that's about ten times heavier than you have used for trout or bass. You can get by with a 10-weight rig under slick, calm conditions, and the lighter line may actually be more effective, but you are going to sacrifice quite a bit during the fight if you don't have a 12-weight with some backbone. There are dozens of excellent tarpon reels on the market today, and the new synthetic braid lines in 50- to 80-pound test make excellent backing. The fly line must be a weight-forward tarpon taper. The only three styles we use are floating, floating with a clear sinking tip, and the clear

Pat Ford's fly box full of Tarpon Toads at the start of the season.

Steve Ward casts to a school of tarpon off Miami.

The Toad is my favorite tarpon fly.

A tarpon sucking in a fly produces the best twenty seconds in fishing.

monocore slime lines. If you have one outfit, stick with a floating line and at least a 10-foot leader. We use 20-pound Mason "hard" monofilament for our fun fishing with an 80-pound fluorocarbon shock tippet. The body of your leader is usually 50- to 60-pound fluorocarbon, but the guide will help you rig up your rod for the actual conditions you will be facing on a particular day. Most of Lefty Kreh's books will show you the rigging and knot styles.

Now that you are armed with a balanced 12-weight outfit that you can cast 60 feet quickly, comfortably, and accurately, you are ready to meet your fish.

If you are looking at a laid-up or motionless tarpon, the fly should land softly about 2½ feet in front of it. I usually let the fly sink slowly, and often the tarpon will simply slide over and inhale it. If there is no immediate response, a smooth, soft slide should do the trick. Be very careful not to have the fly "attack" the fish—they get very upset when a 3-inch bug looks like it wants to bite them. Stripping a fly at the fish or too sharply is all it takes to spook a laid-up tarpon. It's sort of like being asleep and waking up to find a mouse charging at your nose—you don't want the fish's first reaction to be "Yikes."

The longer the fly is in the face of the tarpon, the better your chances are of getting a bite, which is the most exciting in fishing. Normally, a 5-gallon bucket mouth opens and sucks in your fly, but I have seen them clear 3 feet of water, complete with back flips, to get at a fly. Every bite is different and more addictive, but there is one rule: Don't set the hook until the fish closes its mouth and turns its head. Set the hook with a strip strike in the opposite direction to the way the fish turned. If you raise the rod in a typical trout strike, you will lose the fish every time. Fifteen years later after hundreds of missed and caught fish, I know without a doubt that the best way to hook a tarpon, regardless of the kind of bite you get, is to get tight with the fish with the stripping hand before you go to the rod to set the hook. Don't move the rod until you feel the fish with your line hand.

Now cruising fish, especially the strings and schools that move along the Atlantic coast, require a different approach. Oceanside, you are in gin-clear water, often over a light sand bottom. You can spot the strings and wads of tarpon coming a hundred yards away—well, not always, but it is what we hope for. This gives you plenty of time to fall completely to pieces. The fish are huge, averaging 6 feet in length with eyes as big as baseballs. Hopefully, your line will be smoothly coiled in a line tamer and not tangled around your feet or some cleat on the boat. The wind naturally will be blowing over your casting shoulder, trying to implant your hook squarely into your shoulder blade after your second backcast. You might be staked out, or the guide may be poling you into position for that perfect cast.

This is not the way to make a friend of Captain Rick Murphy.

Rick Orcut casts to a school of tarpon off Curtis Point, Miami, as Captain Rick Murphy gives instructions. Curtis Point is named after Captain Bill Curtis, who spent half his life there.

Big fish, little fly.

My tarpon stretcher ready for action.

No matter how good you are in the backyard, the sight of twenty 100-pound tarpon will blow your mind. Get used to it and expect to panic.

When intercepting fish on the "tarpon highway," I always want to cast well before I should. I keep repeating "one cast, one fish" and force myself to wait. I like to have my 70-foot cast lead the fish by 30 feet. If you are ocean fishing, do not cast to the fish; cast to an interception point. You do not want to let the tarpon see the fly hit the water. Let the fly hover in the water and smoothly slide it into position as the tarpon close the distance. I use flies with marabou or Zonker Strip tails a lot because the materials come alive in the water with almost no stripping movement. I try to slowly slide the fly with my line hand

These are two of my all-time favorite tarpon photos.

while twitching the rod tip. By shaking, bumping, and tweaking the fly, I am "talking to the poon," and I don't want to take the food out of his comfort range with a series of 2-foot jerks. If everything goes according to plan, the tarpon will start to rise up in the water and light up—you can just see that its attitude has changed, and it's going to eat. The fish will usually accelerate, suck in the fly, and turn. Time to set the hook and hang on!

Gotcha!

The five seconds prior to the bite to fifteen seconds after are the greatest twenty seconds in fishing. You have just learned that by sliding, bumping, and tweaking the fly, a tarpon can be pulled, teased, and convinced that eating your fly is the right thing to do. Once connected to *megalops*, the fish will get airborne. It will fly, flip, run, bust, dig, and hunker down. Cartwheeling across the surface, its air moves will rattle and roll, and it will run off 100 yards of backing before you can get the motor down. Sometimes they'll blow blood with their violent head shakes. You get the bite, you get the show, and you get religion. Bring on the sleepless nights. There is no better show on the water—anywhere.

I have heard a lot of good anglers tell me how they have fought an 80-pound tarpon for two or three hours. I routinely land 150-pound tarpon in less than twenty

A 130-pound poon about to be released.

Nothing compares to a big tarpon that has just realized it's been hooked. Note the tiny fly in its top lip.

When a tarpon takes to the air, you'd better bow or he'll be gone.

Tarpon candy—the infamous Paloa Worm.

Captain Eric Herstedt holds on to a 120-pound tarpon that doesn't want to pose for a photo.

minutes. Pat Ford figures he has landed twenty tarpon over 140 pounds over the last ten years, and none have taken over thirty minutes. Stu Apte is the absolute master of fighting big tarpon on fly, and his technique is set out in a video he did with Captain Rick Murphy many years ago called *The Quest for Giant Tarpon.* Billy Pate also has an excellent video on tarpon fishing, and they all say the same thing—fight the fish hard right from the beginning. Keep the rod low and to the side, bending the first 3 feet above the handle. Pull in different directions, but always keep the pressure on. If you let the tarpon think he can win, he probably will. It is almost impossible to break a 20-pound tippet while a fish is in the water but watch out when he jumps and starts flipping that 100-pound body around—that's why you have to "bow" to the silver king and take the pressure off the tippet. As soon as he gets back in the water, go after him with heavy, consistent pressure, never allowing him to rest. You have to beat them psychologically as well as physically. You can rest after the fish is released.

You need to set up a tarpon vacation almost a year in advance—seriously! During the peak season, most guides are impossible to get. My guides and dates are set years in advance, and I keep the same guide for the same days—each and every year. It is now a way of life. Try to book at least three days in a row—if not a week. This way, you've got a good chance to see tarpon fishing at its best.

Many of the fly shops all over the country have access to guides or can direct you to them. Make sure you communicate fully with your guide concerning who is responsible for what, and that includes when and where to meet, who brings the lunches, what clothes to wear, who has what equipment, and so on. No questions are "too simple," and naturally the guide will need a deposit if you are not a regular customer.

Good luck and hang on. Sleepless nights won't be far away!

If you want to set up some tarpon fishing, you can call the Biscayne Bay Fly Shop in Miami at (305) 669-5851, Florida Keys Outfitters in Islamorada at (305) 664-5423, the Salt Water Angler in Key West at (305) 294-3248, or call (305) 664-9097 for a copy of the *Redbone Journal,* which has a listing of all the best guides in South Florida.

Baby Tarpon, Redfish, and Snook

CAPTAIN RICK MURPHY

Chico Fernández works a mangrove shoreline in Florida Bay for snook.

Sometimes redfish are nice enough to hang out in clear water.

Over the past twenty years of guiding anglers through the waters of South Florida and the Keys, the one thing I can say without hesitation is that Everglades National Park is one of the most complex ecosystems in the world. The semi-town of Flamingo on the southwest point of Florida's mainland consists of a ranger station, a general store, a motel, a few cottages, a campground, and one restaurant. Flamingo is 28 miles due west of Key Largo, 23 miles northwest of Islamorada, and about 60 miles from both Key West and Miami. The Native Americans called the Everglades the "river of grass" because it is mostly sawgrass, mangrove islands, and water (at least in the rainy summer season), and it literally covers over two million acres. There are no markers on most of its creeks, bays, or ponds, and a novice can easily become confused and most assuredly lost. South of Flamingo in Florida Bay, the going isn't much easier. The entire area is woven with flats and channels that will leave an unobservant boater stranded on a bank with no hope of movement until the tide rises. We call the entire area "Flamingo," and though difficult to learn, its fishing is outstanding for tarpon, snook, redfish, and a dozen other species such as tripletail, black drum, ladyfish, seatrout, grouper, and sharks. I am sure there are places that have bigger tarpon, more redfish, and nastier snook, but there is no place that I have found where you

A perfect time for the flats—dead calm in the late afternoon.

White pelicans migrate to the Everglades by the thousands every winter.

can catch all three in the same day on a fly while gliding through mere inches of water in the midst of dozens of tropical wading birds and even alligators. You can spend a week at Flamingo and never fish the same water twice. You might see another boat, but you won't see many, and there are plenty of fish to go around.

Flamingo is Miami's doorway to Florida Bay and the monster tarpon that guys like Andy Mill and Billy Pate spend a fortune pursuing in the spring, but that topic is covered in Andy's chapter, and I want to introduce you to the fun fishing: baby tarpon, redfish, and snook.

Unfortunately, Flamingo is not a place you can fish on your own successfully on your first trip. You really need a local guide, and there are plenty of great ones in our area. The need for a guide is threefold: (1) he knows his way around the flats, mangroves, and oyster bars; (2) he knows the tides, the patterns the fish follow, and where they were yesterday; and (3) he can pole you through inches of water along mangrove shorelines, spot fish, and put you into position for that perfect cast. You really do need a guide if you want the complete Everglades package.

The best time to fish in Flamingo is late April through November. Even though temperatures can get pretty high down here in July and August, the fishing doesn't suffer—tarpon, redfish, and snook thrive on water temperatures that would boil a bonefish. If you meet your guide at the boat ramp just before daylight and it's already warm, calm, and you are starting to sweat, relax—those conditions are perfect. The calmer it is, the better the fly fish-

Alligators are a common sight in the Hell's Bay area north of Flamingo.

A bald eagle protects his lunch on a tidal flat in Lake Ingrahm.

A summer storm off Cape Sable.

Roseate spoonbills can be found wading in the shallow flats . . .

ing. This is what dreams are made of. On a normal day in the summer, we'll be leaving the dock as soon as darkness begins to break. We might spend some time looking for big tarpon if they've been around, but our real objective will be their baby brothers—tarpon up to 20 pounds or so. Every June, the rains come to south Florida and afternoon thunderstorms flood the Everglades, changing the salinity of the rivers and bays. The water in the inland shallow ponds where the small tarpon winter gradually becomes more fresh than salt, and the native minnows, which are the tarpon's primary food source, move out into the river mouths and the mangroves that rim the ponds, bays, and bights. Tarpon can be seen rolling and splashing by the dozens at first light, and they are usually eager to devour anything that remotely resembles a shrimp or minnow. I have been doing this all my life, and I still get excited, even when I'm not the one fishing.

. . . or just flying by.

I have a number of private places for these early morning poons, but the trick is always to be there at first light—feeding time. I always recommend a 9-weight rod and a floating tarpon or bonefish taper line. Leaders should be at least 10 feet long, and you will need 12 inches of 40-pound fluorocarbon shock tippet. Most of the time the tarpon will be cruising in and out of the edges of the mangroves, and you'll be casting to rolling fish at a distance of about 50 feet. There won't be any long runs involved, so most any saltwater reel will suffice, but you will have to place your fly at the edge of the mangrove roots time and time again. You can probably get by with an 8-weight, but sometimes we throw poppers or bushy flies that are hard to turn over with the lighter rod. Also, these little tarpon are even harder to hook than their big brothers. Their mouths are as hard as bricks, and they don't have enough body weight to counterbalance the hook set. You still have to strip-strike every fish, and the 9-weight improves your hookups considerably. When you find a concentration of these miniature silver kings, the action can be fast and furious. As soon as it feels the hook,

A cluster of great egrets will often mark a shoreline full of baitfish.

Sunrise on Florida Bay.

There is no end to the beauty of the birdlife in the Everglades.
AL FORNS

Ospreys are a common sight on the markers in Florida Bay.

a 2-foot tarpon will jump 4 feet into the air, do several cartwheels, crash back into the water, run 10 yards, and then do it all over again. They are really hard to keep on a hook, but all you are after is that wonderful strike and the magic jumps.

For some reason, the tarpon seem to creep back into the mangroves by nine or ten o'clock at the latest. It is possible to hook a snook once in a while in the midst of the tarpon, but about the time the tarpon quit, the sun is up enough for you to spot the snook laid up under the

A small tarpon released at dawn.

The small summer tarpon are just as much fun as their big brothers and a lot less work.

mangroves or cruising along the edges. However, before too long, it will be time to venture out onto the flats.

There are vast areas of flats outside of Flamingo that hold seatrout, redfish, black drum, and snook. You can barely get a boat up to the fish on low tides. I run a 16-foot Maverick tunnel drive that lets me get most anywhere a redfish can swim, and on a typical day, I run up into Snake Bight until I spot some tailing reds. From that point on, you are in fish city. Redfish are great fun and thankfully relatively angler-friendly (a.k.a. not very bright). Sight-fishing for redfish on the flats is excellent practice for bonefishing. On calm days, you can spot a redfish tail 100 yards away. It's like a shiny red flag beckoning you over

Captain Herstedt's favorite mangrove fly.

A 30-pound tarpon falls to a Mud Toad fly. Everything in Flamingo eats the Mud Toad.

Tarpon from 5 to 20 pounds live along the mangroves during the summer months.

Redfish spend most of the time with their heads buried in the mud and weeds, so put the fly right on their noses.

for some fun. When a red tail is waving in the air, it means that the fish's head is digging something out of the weeds and mud. This is the perfect time to drop a fly right on its nose. If it's a bit breezy, the reds may be cruising or mudding, just like bonefish. When the reds are on the move, you need to lead them by a few feet and try to bring the fly into the fish's feeding zone without spooking it. Redfish are opportunists and will eat most anything that doesn't try to attack them. Many times, we find them following stingrays, gulping down whatever creatures the stingray scares out of hiding. When the reds are on a ray, all the angler has to do is drop the fly on the back end of the ray, which is always an easy target. The only problem is that jack crevalle also follow the rays around and usually beat the redfish

A gold, spotted tail means redfish.

to the fly. When that happens, enjoy it. Jacks put up a great fight.

If the wind picks up during the day in the summer, it's a blessing for the guide and angler. It makes the casting a bit more difficult, and many anglers prefer to step up to a 10-weight, not for the fish, but for the ease of throwing a big fly accurately. Most of our redfish flies are relatively big, bushy, and have bead eyes and weed guards. Sometimes even a 9-weight isn't enough to punch these flies into the wind. It's pretty much an angler preference, but it is wise to have both a 9- and 10-weight fully rigged at all times. Muddlers, deceivers, poppers, crab, minnow, and shrimp patterns all work. My favorite pattern is probably Tim Borski's Chernobyl Shrimp in brown, white, or chartreuse, except in extremely muddy water, where black seems to work best.

We find snook actually mixed in with the reds on the flats. They don't really tail, but can be seen cruising or laid up in potholes. The snook run bigger than the reds and are much harder to fool. The same 9- or 10-weight outfits work fine, and again, a 40-pound fluorocarbon shock tippet is a must. The snook are the prize on Flamingo's flats, unless of course you manage to hook one of the 100-pound tarpon that work their way up into a foot of water every so often. If you want a bigger challenge, there are always sharks to throw at.

One of the best things about fishing out of Flamingo is that you can go south into Florida Bay or north into Whitewater Bay and then west to the rivers that flow into the Gulf or more north into the Hell's Bay area. In the mangrove maze around Whitewater Bay, we usually pole

A southern stingray cruising a grass flat off Sandy Key.

Redfish flies are pretty bushy and sometimes hard to cast on a 7- or 8-weight rod—9- or 10-weight is perfect.

It's not as glamorous as the bonefish, but a redfish is a beautiful creature in its own right and a lot easier to catch.

32

If you want to learn how to catch bonefish, start out with a few days of redfishing.

Chico Fernández put this 15-pound snook in the air off Christian Point.

Tim Borski's Chernyoble Shrimp may be the best fly in Flamingo.

the shorelines looking for reds and snook. The reds are usually cruising, but the snook and tarpon can be spotted half hidden in the mangrove roots waiting for their next meal to come to them. This is a great way to perfect your casting. The guide can hold the skiff a comfortable casting distance off the shoreline while the angler works every nook and cranny with a weedless fly. Naturally, problems arise when a snook lunges out of the twisted debris and nails your fly. If you're lucky, he'll keep going into open water, but more likely than not he will turn around and head right back into the mangroves. This is no place for an 8-pound tippet.

Snook season is closed from June to September, but this is when the big boys hang out at the river mouths and shallow wrecks in schools. It's pretty productive to stake out on an oyster bar on a falling tide and cast an intermediate sinking line with a pilcher or mullet-style fly. You can work the channel just like you would a river up north—casting to the opposite edge and swinging the fly back through the middle. If you find a school of snook, you can have a field day with fish up to 20 pounds. For some reason, the school will continue to work the same general area regardless of how many are hooked. You can have a ball until the tide starts to change.

Hell's Bay is a series of creeks north of Flamingo where the salt water blends with fresh. Again, you can sight-fish snook and redfish in small bays and creek mouths. Unfortunately, many of these creeks are so overgrown and narrow that fly fishing is next to impossible—no room for a backcast. However, in the spring and early summer, snook can be found along the west coast beaches north of Cape Florida. In the early morning hours, they get right up in the light surf and chase baitfish right up onto the shore. It's quite a sight and fantastic fly fishing. Again, minnow-style flies are the most effective, and the size should match whatever batifish is on the day's menu. Personally, I prefer sight-casting to dredging a river mouth, but the biggest snook usually are taken in the rivers, so it's worth a bit of sacrifice once in a while. Fortunately, it doesn't take too long to find out whether the fish are around, especially if you have some live pilchers to use as chum. Inside, outside, north, or south—it's all fun.

The key to any good trip is the adventure and who you share it with. When I discovered Flamingo many years ago, I had the benefit of being taught by the best—Stu Apte and Al Pflueger Jr. Stu is absolutely the best tarpon fisherman I have ever known. We have been fishing together since the late 1980s, and he taught a lot of what

A perfect collection of snook flies tied by Ashley Cornelius of Homestead, Florida.

Double-digit snook are found in a foot of water in Snake Bight.

Snooks have big mouths, big appetites, and very sharp gill plates.

On the flats, there's nowhere for a snook to go but up!

Even the small snook are a challenge on fly.

I now use on the flats every day. Al Pflueger was simply amazing with a fly rod, especially for redfish and snook. Al still isn't a man of many words, but when he spoke, I listened and listened carefully for many years. I can never repay Stu and Al for everything they did for me, but now I have two kids of my own who are just beginning to be able to spot a redfish cruising across the skinny waters of Snake Bight or a tarpon sucking down a shrimp floating off Christian Point at dawn. What do I do on my days off? I take them fishing in Everglades National Park.

If you want to fish Everglades National Park, call Captain Eric Herstedt at (954) 592-1228, Captain Tony Tradd at (305) 246-0051, Captain Brian Helms at (305) 815-0617, Captain Rick Murphy at (305) 951-2557, or Captain Dave Denkert at (305) 852-1425.

A tripletail is a flats bonus. This one ate the Mud Toad while we were looking for tarpon.

Tuna and More

PAT FORD

Fishing in the Gulf north of Key West always starts with the shrimp boats.

Blackfin tuna can be caught in both oceans.

I think that if I had two weeks to fish anywhere in the United States, with light tackle not just fly rods, I would undoubtedly go to Key West, Florida. I have fished Key West since the Navy sent me there in 1971, and I still have not done everything it has to offer. The flats from Marathon to the Marquesas offer superb fishing for permit, tarpon, bonefish, and huge sharks, but those species are covered in other chapters in great detail. When I think of Key West, I am reliving days offshore on the wrecks and reefs in the Atlantic and Gulf of Mexico that provide a variety of light tackle and fly fishing that is hard to match anywhere in the world, much less the continental United States.

If Key West has a "season," it probably begins when temperatures drop up north, and the fish begin to migrate south. Sailfish show up in catchable numbers in November, but December is far more exciting. Blackfin and yellowfin tuna suddenly appear just outside the Atlantic reef line. Light-tackle guides like Captain "RT" Trosset, whom I have fished with for some thirty years, run center-console boats that average 30 feet in length and can smoothly navigate most any sea condition. A typical day in December with RT begins with chasing bait—pilchers to be exact. Once

A day in the Atlantic starts with a cast-net.

The shallow wrecks west of the Marquesas are loaded with permit, cuda, and cobia.

located on the edges of the flats and captured, these 3-inch minnows become the best chum a cast-net can provide. All the light-tackle boats have massive live wells that will hold thousands of baits that are casually thrown over the side over the reef, bar, or wreck selected for the day's adventure. Incredibly, the disoriented pilchers stay close to the boat and soon attract most everything in the area. It is not unusual to have wahoo, kingfish, and sailfish crash baits just behind the boat in addition to tuna, cero mackerel, barracuda, and amberjacks.

If an angler enjoys live baiting with 6-, 8-, or 12-pound test tackle, the options are almost unlimited, but

You never can have too many pilchers in Key West.

Matching the pilcher hatch.

This king hit a Rapala for Ted Lund, but they also hit flies regularly. TED LUND

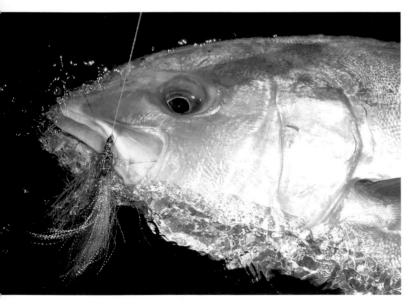

Amberjacks can be teased to the surface like barracuda, but they are no easy catch on a fly rod.

fly fishing is another story altogether and can be wildly rewarding. You really need a 12-weight rod and a large-capacity reel for offshore Key West. Anything lighter is going to create problems sooner or later, and when the yellowfins appear, even the 12-weights will be too light. It is not necessary to cast a great distance, but tuna, wahoo, and sails are all known for their eyesight, and an intermediate clear monocore line has a real advantage, as does a fluorocarbon leader. If the mackerel and wahoo show up, obviously you need to switch to a wire leader, but even light wire pretty much eliminates the tuna strikes. Actually, all you have to do is cast out 30 feet or so behind the boat into a bunch of freshly dumped pilchers and

A selection of offshore flies for Key West.

Not much is safe from a hungry cuda, and they are fantastic sport for a fly rod.

hang on. Every day is different. You never know what will appear behind the boat. It is not unusual to see grouper, snapper, and African pompano right on the surface—if it eats pilchers, it will show up sooner or later.

For reasons unknown, the blackfins seem to slow down in January, but the sailfishing is excellent, and schools of kingfish appear in both oceans. When the kings move into the Gulf, the fishing can be spectacular north and west of the Marquesas. If pilchers are available, they are still the best, but an ordinary block chum line with glass minnows will bring smoker kings into fly-rod range once you find the school. Again, the clear monocore line works best, but a full fast-sinking line can be just as effective if the fish are holding deep. A 30-pound king on a fly rod is a handful even on a 12-weight. If the kings are

RT teases a barracuda for Dr. Randee Ward next to Cosgrove light.

Life as a small jack in Key West is not an easy one.

Schools of big jack crevalles can be found to the west and north of Key West.

being difficult, there are dozens of wrecks scattered all over the Gulf that hold cobia, amberjack, snappers, jacks, cero mackerel, and cuda, all of which can be chummed up into fly-rod range. Oddly, each wreck will hold different opportunities, so if one is slow, just go to another one.

The kingfish can hang around through March, but in February, cobia move in and take over the wrecks and towers in the Gulf. Permit move onto the wrecks also and can be found all the way to the Dry Tortugas. I recall fish-

Here's a 22-pound permit taken off a shallow wreck near the Marquesas.

Captain RT Trosset works up the bonito behind a shrimper.

ing with RT Trosset on some wrecks west of the Marquesas when the cobia and big cudas were stacked up like cordwood. It was March 5, 1985, and I caught a 67-pound 4-ounce cobia on a fly with an 8-pound-test tippet, which is still an IGFA record twenty years later. We also set an IGFA record for a 25-pound 8-ounce barracuda on 4-pound tippet that same trip. Both fish were teased to the surface with a line blue runner and "hand picked" out of a school. Fishing the wrecks is a very visual experience, to say the least.

April through June is probably the best time to fish in Key West, other than the tuna run in December. There are still lots of cobia, amberjacks, and permit on the Gulf wrecks. The key to this fishing is again teasing and chumming, but in March in the Gulf the best source of chum is the shrimp-boat fleet. Dozens of shrimpers drag their nets along the Gulf's flat sand bottom, scooping up every form of creature imaginable. At dawn, the shrimpers haul their nets on board, dump the nets' contents on the deck, and begin sorting out the shrimp from the by-catch. When the shrimp are collected, the "trash" is casually dumped back into the sea. About twenty-five years ago, we discovered that in April and May schools of bonita and blackfin tuna followed the shrimpers around feasting on the

RT and I with a small cobia. We set an IGFA record in 1985 with a 67 1/4-pound cobia on 8-pound tippet that still stands.

Even a small shark can ruin your catch.

creatures stirred up by their nets. Evidently, these predators figured out that if they hang around the anchored shrimp boat for a while, all the food in the nets that disappeared into the sky eventually comes back into the water. Catching tuna behind the shrimp boats is probably my favorite thing to do in Key West in the spring. Many IGFA records on little tunny have been taken behind the shrimpers, and the blackfins can exceed 30 pounds. Fishing these speedsters behind a shrimp boat is like a giant video game. The trick is to hook the blackfins and avoid the bonita, which will outnumber the tuna ten to one. Again, a 12-weight rod is best, but the fly line is immaterial. Casts are rarely 20 feet long, and a white fly is usually struck the instant it hits the water. I use my oldest and most battered fly lines for this, since you can't chase the fish, and a trip around the shrimp boat's rigging or anchor

Bonito behind a shrimp bait can range up to 20 pounds, and the blackfins can get over 30 pounds.

RT's Bump Fly works for everything that responds to shrimp-boat chum.

line will mess up a new line pretty quickly. There have been many days in Key West when we have met the shrimpers at dawn and stayed with them until the afternoon before venturing off to see what was on the wrecks. The fishing can be fantastic.

Permit school around the wrecks and probably spawn out there in March and September. Sometimes, they can be seen milling around the surface or flashing just beneath it. Permit respond to shrimp-boat chum readily, but many times, especially on the Navy Towers, all you need to do is anchor up and wait for the school to swim by. Most of the time, these are big fish exceeding 30 pounds in 70 feet of water, which makes catching them a lot more strenuous than it is on the flats or the shallow wrecks west of the Marquesas. You can catch permit on the shallow wrecks with a 10-weight rod, but at the towers, when a bruiser goes down 50 feet and turns sideways, you will wish you had a 12-weight. Long casts can be very helpful when the permit are cruising, so a full monocore or full sinking striper line is needed. The best fly is naturally some form of Merkin crab pattern.

As spring turns to summer, the light-tackle guides still find permit on the Gulf wrecks, and there is spectacular

Captain Greg Sherertz holds up a nice blackfin tuna for Vidian Mallard.

A wreck permit, west of the Marquesas.

Key West's Pier House provides classic sunsets every night.

Iridescent African pompano are a rare but possible fly catch in December. TED LUND

bottom fishing all the way to the Dry Tortugas, but most guides spend their time chasing dolphin in the Atlantic. Guides like Captain Trosset don't actually troll for dolphin, they run and hunt for weed lines, debris, birds—anything that will signal fish. Once found, the dolphin can be chummed with pilchers and easily induced to take a fly. The only downside is that August can be pretty hot in the Keys.

In September and October, Florida's unsettled weather—i.e., hurricane season—can put a damper on the offshore fishing until the sailfish begin to appear in November. Fortunately, the flats fishing for bonefish and permit in the early fall is outstanding. The biggest bonefish of the year are caught in September and October. There is always something to do with a fly rod in Key West.

If you want to book a light-tackle offshore guide in Key West, you can call Captain RT Trosset directly at (305) 294-5801 or Hurricane Hole Outfitters toll-free at (866) 293-9550 (h2okeywest.com).

Sharks

CAPTAIN "RT" TROSSET AND CAPTAIN TED LUND

Sharks over 200 pounds are hard to control on fly tackle . . .

. . . and a lot of work!

The sun was just about overhead, and it was early April. We had been drifting the flats on the northwest corner of the Marquesas for several hours, only we weren't looking for bonefish, tarpon, or permit—Pat Ford and I were looking for sharks for a fly-rod entry in the Metropolitan Miami Sportfishing Tournament. Although it was over twenty-five years ago, I still remember that day and the great fish that became permanently etched in my mind: a humongous dark shape heading toward my 20-foot seacraft with deadly conviction. It was a bull shark zeroing in on the barracuda carcass we were using as chum. In 4½ feet of water, a shark 12 feet long and 5 feet across from pec to pec and 4 feet from belly to dorsal sort of stands out. The thing had to be over 600 pounds.

Pat had been standing on the bow for an hour pulling his fly away from sharks we didn't deem worthy. My first thought was "Please don't hook this guy," but it was too late. As the fish neared the boat, I could see the cobias escorting him, hoping for scraps—they were all over 30 pounds. Naturally, Pat made a cast, placing the bright orange fly some 40 feet from the boat. Sharks hone in on prey with their nose; the trick is to transfer their brain from scent to sight, and the bright orange fly does the trick better than any other color. Bursting through its cobia posse, the huge shark rolled its head back, ate the fly, and continued toward the boat as Pat set the hook into a quarter ton of bull shark. With a fish that big, the International Game Fish Association's 12-inch wire shock tippet offers little protection. But as one of the world's top light-tackle anglers, Pat fought the shark hard for twenty minutes. As is habit with the large predators, the bull tried to get to shallower water—it knew it was in trouble, and a fish that big was likely to have few enemies in the shallows. When it couldn't go any further, the great fish turned and charged the boat.

Knowing this might be the only chance we'd have at boating the fish, I went for the gaff. Pat was able to lay the fish up parallel to the skiff just long enough for me to get a shot on it. I was holding a 6-foot gaff with only a 3-inch bite, but as soon as I got a piece of the great fish's shoulders, it went under the boat, taking the gaff—and nearly me—with it. The shaft bent, and the gaff hook pulled out of the fish. As it went under the boat, the tippet caught on the keel and parted underneath the hull. Actually, I think we both were relieved as the huge bull shark swam off.

That caliber of shark is rarely seen on the flats anymore. But excitement can still be had by shark fishing in shallow water—anywhere the men in gray suits are found.

Captain Rick Murphy releasing a 300-pound lemon shark Pat Ford caught on fly.

Most of my anglers that experience this type of fishing and successfully release one of the toothy predators often leave feeling more like survivors than victors. In all honesty, the smaller sharks under 150 pounds are the most fun. The big boys are too much work.

The origin of shark fishing on the flats was born of the egos of light-tackle anglers in South Florida like Norman Duncan and Ralph Delph. They are among the largest fish ever taken on regulation fly tackle—even larger than the billfish that have been taken to date. Over the years, I have had the opportunity to develop and fine-tune light-tackle techniques for a number of species. But it was Pat Ford who taught me how to shark fish. Pat was one of the few who knew how to do it, but didn't have the boat or person to gaff the fish, so he showed me everything he knew about it. Our testing grounds were the shallow waters surrounding Key West, but anglers with access to shallow water inhabited by sharks anywhere in South Florida can enjoy it just the same.

I was very fortunate to have the opportunity to make a living and at the same time get an education from anglers like Ford and fellow angler Dr. Scott Russell. Over the years, I have improved upon what we knew twenty-five years ago, and I am glad that with the help of Ted Lund, editor of *Fly Fishing in Salt Waters* magazine, I can share my experiences with the readers of Pat's book.

The popular misconception about shark fishing is that you have to flood the water with blood and guts à la Peter Benchley's Captain Quint. While that may be true in deeper water, a consistent scent path in shallow water created by a single favorite food fish can drive even the largest sharks wild.

When I talk about large sharks in shallow water, consider this: In less than 10 feet of water, I have landed bull sharks to 468 pounds, lemon sharks to 314, hammerhead

Sharks are dangerous creatures to have next to the boat— be careful.

Marty Arostegui revives his world-record lemon shark. We don't recommend this method unless we really don't like the angler. MARTY AROSTEGUI

A 100-pound blacktip shark is as tough as any fish that swims.

sharks to 398, and tiger sharks to 480, but I have also lost tigers and hammers in shallow water that challenged the 1,000-pound mark. In fact, the biggest tiger I've seen in shallow water, we didn't have the chance to lose. In 6 feet of water, the fish's back was out of the water, and it was kicking up mud to get to us. No one wanted to catch it.

In the Lower Keys, barracuda is the favored bait of choice, but anglers in other locations do well with local favorites like jack crevalle, ladyfish, and even stingrays. Any abundant food species will usually attract them, and in a pinch, a block of ground, frozen chum will work for smaller species like lemon and blacktip sharks.

Probably the three most important factors in successful shark fishing on the flats are wind, tide, and temperature conditions. First and foremost, I prefer a wind against the tide situation. While you generally don't want this when anchored, for drifting it gives you the best overall coverage—the wind is pushing your boat along, and the tide is carrying the bait's scent trail away from the boat in a direct line. The lower stages of the outgoing tide seem to be better.

If fishing on the higher stages of the tide, you could be fishing on the crown or middle of a flat, whereas on the lower stages of the tide, all of the shark's favorite foods are swept off the edge of the flat, where they are more likely to be hunting and on the prowl. With regard to water temperature, anything below 72 degrees and the fish behave really funky; from 76 to 78 degrees, they are pretty active; anything much over 88 degrees and you lose most species except for lemon sharks. For the most part, we have excellent fishing for sharks year-round, but the biggest ones show up between February and May.

Regardless of the type of tackle you are using, it is best to hook the shark on its first run toward the boat. You need to be aware the fish is coming, because on that first charge, they are coming in to eat. On subsequent visits, they become more and more wary. It is easy to be lulled into complacency waiting for fish to come into the chum, but you can't let down your guard. It is hard to believe that a 400-pound fish can sneak up on your boat in 4 feet of water, but they do—routinely. Usually, they leave with your chum, which is why it is a good idea to not put all your cudas or ladyfish out at once. If fishing fly or other artificials, anglers must anticipate the shark's movements. Make the presentation in front of the fish and to the side so you can move it and make sure they can see it. A shark's eyesight is not very good, and it's important to put the lure where they will intercept it.

When trying to catch these—and other big fish—on fly, the most important thing you can do is to watch which side of the fish's mouth the hook comes to rest in. If you can figure that out and fight the fish from that side, your chances of success increase dramatically.

I first learned that lesson when fishing with marine artist Mike Stidham a number of years ago. After hooking and losing about twenty-five hammerhead sharks on fly tackle, I decided that we needed to shove the rod tip underwater and bring the 12 inches of shock tippet—all that's allowed under IGFA rules—under and behind the hammer of the fish. Stidham executed the move perfectly and after forty minutes, I gaffed and boated the first ever hammerhead taken on IGFA fly tackle.

The majority of the fishing we do for sharks is with the fly rod because of the growing popularity of the sport. The fish are cooperative and generally aren't too picky about presentation—a perfect combination for those wanting to learn how to fly-fish in saltwater. Any high-quality 12-weight or larger rod will do. In all of my fly fishing offshore, I believe in using heavier rods. While there are situations you can get away with a 9- or 10-weight, invariably as soon as you limit yourself to smaller tackle, a 200-pound fish will charge the boat. Floating lines work best, as they keep the fly out of the seagrass and up in the water column, but I like to modify the line by cutting back the length to 80 feet off the back. This allows me to pack the reel with additional backing and reduces the drag created by the fly line, letting anglers put more direct pressure on fish. For backing, I prefer the Spectra-type lines in 60-

Getting your fly back can be a problem.

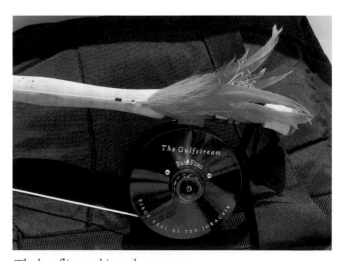

The best flies are big and orange.

Maneuvering a shark for a photo has to be done carefully.

Sometimes the shark and the guide have the same expressions.

pound test, which is equivalent in diameter to 20-pound Dacron. It will also make short work of any lobster or crab trap buoys if your fish should swim around one.

With regard to flies, any color will work as long as it is orange. I don't know why, but over the years, orange has proven to be the best color. The fish seem to like it, and it is very easy for the angler and guide to see. Large deceiver-style patterns work best especially when tied on a 5/0 3407 SS double-strength hook.

Over the years, I have developed some different ideas about the terminal tackle required of sharks. Obviously, because of the nature of the beast, wire is a necessity to prevent bite-offs. For fly and artificial lure applications, I finally settled on 45- to 60-pound-test Steelon. Not only does the material lend itself to easier knot-tying, but the multi-strand wire fits in the gap between the teeth of most sharks, preventing them from chewing through the shock trace. For the class tippet, I prefer a "hard," abrasion-resistant monofilament, such as Rio or Mason, in line tests up to 20 pounds for IGFA and tournament purposes. You lose very few fish to chaffing with "hard"-type tippet material. In classic tippet construction form, I'll double each end of the line with a Bimini Twist, leaving a single strand of tippet about 2 feet in length in between the knots. I'll tie a Surgeon's Loop in one of the doubles, which will connect to the butt section and connect the other end of the tippet to the braided wire with either an Albright Special or Triple Surgeon's Knot.

Usually in shallow water, hooked sharks will head even shallower. It is important to keep pressure on the fish at all times and to be alert about the attitude of the fish. One thing that most species of sharks have in common is that they will attack the boat when they feel threatened. Pulitzer Prize–winning author and former Key West resident Phil Caputo tells a story of being thrown into the water by a famous Key West captain who jammed his boat into reverse to avoid the wrath of an onrushing 300-pound bull shark. "The next thing I knew, I was the only thing between a 300-pound bull shark and the boat," Caputo said. "I did a standing leap back in the boat and never got wet above my knees. Fear is a great motivator." Try to avoid putting yourself in that position.

Today there is really no reason to kill a shark, and it is a simple matter of breaking the fish off at the boat. If you want to get a picture of your catch, which we often do with blacktips and lemon sharks, a tailer like those made by Aftco will allow you to get control of the fish, remove it from the water for a few quick snapshots, then release it to fight another day, but be careful—they bite!

Shark fishing on the flats is available from Miami to Key West and throughout Florida Bay. The biggest are actually off the oceanside of Key Largo and in Key West, but Florida Bay is full of lemons, blacktips, bull sharks, and a few surprises. On St. Patrick's Day in 1999, Pat Ford was fishing for sharks with Captain Rick Murphy and Joe Rodriguez out of Flamingo. Actually, they started

Tiger sharks are the ultimate fly-rod catch on the flats. Artist Tim Borski would rather catch tigers than tarpon.

A tailer is considerably easier on the shark than a gaff.

A 250-pound tiger shark has little fear of the boat or anything else.

Big nurse sharks are easily chummed in off Key West, but they don't have the best eyesight and rely mostly on smell. They are also extremely stupid.

the day tarpon fishing and gradually gave up, caught a few ladyfish, and starting sharking. Pat caught a few lemons, and after a lull of about an hour, a big boy appeared in the chum. It picked up speed as the ladyfish scent grew stronger, and just as it got into casting range, they both realized it had stripes—a tiger shark. At that time, the IGFA world record for tiger sharks on 15-pound tippet was only in the 100-pound range. This fish was close to 200 pounds. As Rick Murphy tells the story, Pat hooked up as usual and fought the fish hard; the only problem was they didn't have a gaff—only the tailer I mentioned earlier. Pat would get the shark up to the boat, Rick would run up with the tailer and try to lasso it, only to have the tiger take off. This went on and on for half an hour until the tippet parted. While Pat was dejected, Murphy went into action. Another tippet was attached and they raced back up onto the flat where the shark had been last seen and dumped the ladyfish over again. Tiger sharks are not particularly bright, by the way, and are afraid of nothing. All they think about is food.

As the story goes, ten minutes later up pops the same tiger shark and makes a beeline for the ladyfish. Pat cast out the new fly, the shark ate the fly again, and off they went again. After another ten minutes, the shark was back up along the side of the boat, and on the third pass, Rick got the loop around the shark's tail. After that, all they had to do was drag it into Murphy's Hewes Redfisher without getting maimed themselves. That was the only shark Pat has killed since probably 1980, but it weighed 196.5 pounds and is still an IGFA world record. Not bad for a couple of Irishmen from Miami on St. Patrick's Day. Murphy had the shark mounted for his patio, where it hangs today.

Over the years, I have not only had a great deal of fun and excitement catching sharks on the flats, but there is no better way to teach an angler how to fight a big fish on a fly rod. I have had them chew the spray rails off my boat, leave their teeth in the gunwales off my flats skiff, and even chew on my propeller, but I keep coming back for more. Even today, there are few fish that get me as excited as shallow-water sharks. Give it a try, and I will bet you'll be as hooked as I am. It's a rush!

If you want to fish for sharks in the Miami–Key Largo area, call Eric Herstedt at (954) 592-1228 or Captain Gary Spence at (305) 235-5580 (Sharkmastercharters.com). In Key West, call Captain RT Trossett at (305) 294-5801. To see shark fishing at its best, watch Captain Rick Murphy's *Sportsman's Adventures* show on the Sunshine Network.

Butterfly Peacock Bass and Other Exotics

MARTY AROSTEGUI

Sunrise on a Miami lake is prime time for fly-fishing shorelines.

Butterfly peacock bass cruise the shorelines and docks of most Miami lakes and canals.

I nterested in fishing for world records? Catching a world record these days doesn't happen by accident. World-record fishing requires angling skill, knowledge of International Game Fish Association (IGFA) rules, and the proper tackle, as well as a specific target in mind.

Forget about the very popular species such as tarpon, bonefish, permit, and snook. So many good anglers target these species that the records for these fish are extremely difficult to attain. The best opportunities for records are in some of the less popular fish that have been designated by the IGFA as eligible for line-class world-record consideration.

The best and only way to become familiar with which fish to target is to become a member of the IGFA. Membership includes an annual publication, *The World Record Game Fishes*, which lists all the species of fish available for records as well as all current records and angling rules and regulations for line class and fly rod. Membership also gives you access to the IGFA Web site, where all recent applications are posted as pending records.

By accessing the free IGFA Web site, you can get up-to-date information, which is essential since the yearbook listings may be surpassed at any time.

Once you review the list of potential records, a number of very exotic destinations will come to mind: Venezuela or Brazil for peacocks, South America for oscars, Central America for jaguar and clown knifefish-guapote, Malasia for snakeheads—or you can book a flight to South Florida and

South Florida has thousands of miles of canals that provide some extremely unusual fish for Captain Alan Zaremba.

Steve Kantner, a.k.a. "the land captain," holds up a clown knifefish caught in Broward County. How these fish got there is anyone's guess.

target all of these species by simply fishing from southern Miami to northern Fort Lauderdale.

No, I am not crazy! South Florida is home to multiple exotic species that are on the list of world-record fishes. You wonder how I know? Well, I have over thirty IGFA world records for exotic fish caught in the canals of South Florida.

Many years ago, most of South Florida was everglades. In order to develop the land and build homes, an intricate system of canals was dug out to provide proper water drainage and prevent our homes from being flooded during the rainy season.

The canal system of South Florida became the perfect habitat for many exotics that were inadvertently released over the years. Approximately 20 years ago, tilapia took so well to Florida waters that they were crowding out most of the native species in the canal systems. After many studies, the Florida Game and Fresh Water Fish Commission, under the direction of biologist Paul L. Shafland, introduced the butterfly peacock (*Cichla ocellaris*) to increase predation on the tilapia and other non-native species, and there was a slight hope that the peacocks would enhance freshwater fishing opportunities in South Florida.

The peacocks are now well-established and have grown enough that multiple world records in line class and fly rod have been caught in South Florida canals. Butterfly peacocks can be found from southern Dade County to northern Broward County. Most canals and lakes have them in

Jeff Harkavy releases a 40-pound pacu for his daughter Heather, age ten.

The bullseye snakehead is the latest menace to appear in Florida.

good numbers, and they can be fished from a boat or by walking and casting from the side of most canals.

Keeping company with the butterfly peacocks are a number of other exotics that can be targeted for world records: oscars, jaguar guapote, mayan cichlids, tilapia, midas cichlids, and more recently, even clown kingfish and the unwanted bullseye snakehead have appeared in surprising numbers.

Today, there are a few guides in South Florida that actually target the freshwater exotics. The best captains are Alan Zaremba and Jim Anson. These two guides are responsible for a large percentage of all the world records caught in South Florida. If you are interested in an exotic urban fishing experience, I suggest you call one of them and book a trip. Spring, summer, and fall are good times to fish, with spring being the best time. The daily weather has very little effect on the fishing, which makes it very reliable, but there's actually plenty to catch in the winter too.

Blue tilapia are a rare fly-rod catch. MARTY AROSTEGUI

Florida's butterfly peacocks have different markings than those in the Amazon.

Peacocks are very popular fish, and already many anglers travel to South Florida to fish for them. In the spring, the peacocks start spawning in large numbers, and the larger fish are most vulnerable. The same holds true for the other exotics as well.

The best world-record opportunities are on light lines and the fly tippets such as 2-, 4-, 6-, 8-, and 12-pound test. Remember that there must be at least 15 inches of class tippet, and the shock section cannot exceed 12 inches, knot to fly. A light spinning rod with an ultralight reel will work well for the light lines and a 6- to 8-weight fly rod will suffice for most fly-fishing opportunities. The fly fisherman should bring floating line and bright-colored Clouser Minnow patterns with weed guards. Small plugs work best for casting with a spinning rod, but there is no substitute for a live shiner. It is also wise to use IGFA-certified test lines, such as Ande Tournament or Rio. If your line overtests, you don't get the record, so it's actually smart to test your line before tying the tippets.

For those interested in catching a potential world record, there are other important considerations. The IGFA requires that the application be completely filled in and signed by your guide and witnesses, so it is best to bring blank copies along to facilitate the process at the end of the fishing day. The IGFA also requires that all fish be weighed with a certified scale on land and measured. This requirement is best accomplished by purchasing a portable spring scale and sending it to the IGFA for certification, which lasts for one

Oscars made the transition from fish tank to canal very easily.

Jaguar guapote somehow made it from the South American jungles to South Florida.

There are few fish as colorful as Miami's peacock bass.

Red midas cichlids take on a variety of color combinations.

Even the creatures along the shore are exotic.

year. I strongly recommend a Boga Grip scale because, in my estimation, it is the most reliable of the small scales on the market, and it will recertify year after year. A small camera is essential because you must submit one or more photos that show the angler holding the fish with the rod and reel used for the catch and the scale used to weigh the fish. I usually accomplish this requirement by jumping onto the canal bank and having my photo taken while holding the fish with the Boga Grip scale in one hand and the rod and reel with the other hand. This way, one photo accomplishes all the basic requirements, but it is also wise to include a photo of the fish lying on a tape measure, which can be done on the boat. I also take a net with a long handle (less than 8 feet) to facilitate the landing of the fish.

It's hard to believe a fish is actually this color or this shape. MARTY AROSTEGUI.

Peacocks guard their young from the local largemouth bass for weeks. Check out the bass in the upper left corner of the photo.

During a record catch, I follow this sequence: Once the fish is landed, I determine if the weight is enough to surpass or tie the current record. If the fish is determined to be a potential record, we measure the fish, note the length and girth, jump on the canal bank to determine the accurate weight, and take a photo with all the previously noted requirements. Remember that the guide, not the angler, must confirm the weight, and a second witness is a plus. I take a small notebook on the boat to write down all necessary information in order to facilitate the filing of the application later. We then release the fish. Keeping the fish alive is very important. If we leave a glitch in the process, we have a live fish that can be placed in the live well until we get our act together. Many people do not realize that there is no reason to kill a fish just so it can be a record.

South Florida is a great place to visit. We have vibrant multiethnic communities that foster great restaurants, museums, art exhibits, and some of the most beautiful beaches in the world. Covered in snow? Come to our tropical environment, and leave your cold weather problems behind. You might just go home with an IGFA world record to impress your snowbound friends.

You can reach Alan Zaremba at (954) 961-0877 and Jim Anson at (305) 235-6304 and the International Game Fish Association at IGFA.org.

Marty Arostegui holds up an IGFA-record butterfly peacock . . .

. . . and then releases it. There is no need to kill a fish for an IGFA record anymore.

Trout

PAT FORD

A sand glacier lies just above the Lee's Ferry crossing.

Someone once told me that trout are extremely intelligent fish because they live in such beautiful places. I know it's hard to compare the fight of a typical spring-creek rainbow to that of most any saltwater fish, but the art of fly-fishing for trout is, very simply, a great deal of fun. I grew up trout fishing in New York and New Jersey, but I drifted away from it once I moved to Florida and discovered bonefish and tarpon. As I grew older and less fanatical, I began to look for interesting places to take vacations where my family could relax and I could fish. We have been to a number of streams and rivers over the years, and I have caught my share of western trout and loved every minute of it. There are hundreds of great trout streams out West, but I can safely say that I have two favorite areas.

Bozeman, Montana, is a charming college town where the people are friendly, the skies are clean, and the fishing is superb. Any local guide shop can fix you up with a float trip on the Yellowstone or Madison rivers, but the jewels of this area are the spring creeks and the private ponds. You can travel in most any direction from Bozeman and find a variety of great trout fishing, which makes it an excellent base of operations.

During my dozen or so visits to Bozeman, I have fished with Alan Gadoury who runs 6X Outfitters. Alan special-

This Montana cutthroat fell for a dry fly fished along the shoreline of a lake just outside Bozeman.

A summer shower over Depuy Spring Creek.

The top end of Nelson Spring Creek is a prime spot for cutthroat trout.

izes in trips to the spring creeks just outside Livingston—Nelson, Depuy, and Armstrong. He has access to half a dozen others, but these are the "big three." It is difficult for a tourist to purchase rod space on Depuy or Armstrong and almost impossible to get one on Nelson. Alan has several days a week personally booked on these elite creeks, and if you want to fish them, the only way is to go through him or possibly one of the local fly shops, but you must make the reservations months in advance.

Nelson Spring Creek is reconstructed each year to provide optimal trout habitat.

The spring creeks are extremely difficult to fish, but there are mayfly hatches all summer and the dry-fly fishing can be spectacular. The creeks themselves vary in depth, current, and width, but generally you should be fishing a 2- to 4-weight rod and a 6X tippet. Local guides like Alan know far more about which fly to use at which time than I will ever comprehend. Somehow these trout, which all have PhDs as far as I'm concerned, know the difference between a size 16 and a size 18 Pale Morning Dun, and whether they are feeding on PMDs or sulphurs or spinners. You will need chest-high Gore-Tex waders, but the wading itself is quite easy and safe. You can expect to catch rainbows, browns, and cutthroats on any given day. Naturally, there is a rod fee, but it is well worth the price, as is the knowledge of a guide like Alan.

Fly fishing in the Bozeman area starts in March when the weather is cold and windy, but if it warms up at mid-day and the winds lie down, you can have a few hours of great success with nymphs, midges, and blue-winged olives on creeks with no weeds and no people. Obviously, the fishing improves in April and May, as does the weather. Blue-winged olives and midges hatch on the spring creeks, and around the first of May the caddis begin to hatch on the Yellowstone, which is the best dry-fly fishing on the river all year. Lakes ice out in late April, hopefully, and this

The slow sections of Depuy and Armstrong spring creeks provide exceptional dry-fly fishing.

Armstrong Spring Creek—paradise valley, Montana.

A pale morning dunn and a PMD, matching the hatch.

6X tippets and size 16 nymphs work on big fish too.

is the best time to land a double-digit rainbow. In June, the salmon flies start hatching on the large freestone rivers. Predicting the exact date of a hatch is next to impossible due to runoff and changing weather, but some anglers devote their lives to catching a salmon fly hatch in Montana.

July is absolutely the best time to fish Montana. Pale morning duns hatch on the spring creeks, and there is great dry-fly action on the lakes with damsel flies and *Callibaetis*. As soon as the big rivers clear the runoff, the trout start looking up for hoppers. August is pretty much the same, but the spring-creek trout get a bit more difficult to fool. There are good sulphur hatches in the afternoons, Tricos peak on the Missouri, and the hopper fishing on the Yellowstone is excellent!

September and October offer the best midge hatches of the season on the spring creeks, but the big trout hunter

The heavy weed growth provides rich insect life and daily hatches on the spring creeks.

will be fishing streamers on the Yellowstone and Missouri rivers in the midst of spectacular fall foliage. After October, you really need to enjoy cold weather a lot to want to go fishing in the snow.

A few days on a Montana spring creek will hone your trout skills to perfection, but if you want big fish, your best bet would be to visit one of the private ponds in the area. Again, the ponds will require a rod fee, and you will need a guide just to find them. One of my favorites is a pond full of cutthroats on a ranch in Big Timber where

A beautifully colored spring-creek brown.

A rare sight—a hook-jawed lake rainbow, 28 inches long.

The small creeks leading into the Gallatin River sometimes hold some pretty big fish. NEAL ROGERS

My wife, Kay, has her own approach to pond fishing.

the prime food source is damselflies and you fish from float tubes. Other ponds require boats, but some can effectively be fished from shore, such as Swamp Lake and Diving Buffalo. My preference on the ponds is a 4- to 6-weight rod, since longer casts are helpful and the leaders don't have to be as light. In addition, there are dozens of lakes available to anglers, and fishing on each is different. As expected, the best source of information is the local fly shop that is arranging your trip. They always know what area is hot at any particular time.

Depending on the lake or pond, trout can run up to 10 pounds, but it is usually best to fish them early in the season before the water temperature gets too high. Too much stress in warm water can be fatal to a fat rainbow.

In spite of all this, my absolute favorite place to fish in all of Montana, if not the world, is on a friend's ranch in Big Sky. Unfortunately (or fortunately) this particular

A collection of spring creek and pond flies.

place is not open to the public. Stu Apte introduced me to Chuck Anceny about a dozen years ago, and since then we have become good friends. I have spent some fantastic fishing hours on Chuck's ranch. Chuck turned ninety-one in August 2005 and still is the ultimate cowboy. He grew up on a horse and still rides several times a week. His property has been in his family for decades, and he tells how sixty years ago his grandfather diverted two spring creeks into a pond and then let the pond drain into the Gallatin River. Back in the 1940s, his family enlarged the pond and decided to raise foxes, mink, and beavers for their pelts. As Chuck tells the tail, the first thing that happened was that the beavers killed all the mink and foxes, then ate all the aspens, then finally ate all the fence posts and escaped. So much for fur farming! Today, Chuck treats his pond as a giant aquarium, raising rainbows and browns over 30 inches in length in a crystal-clear spring-creek environment. I'm afraid not even an autographed copy of this book would get you onto Chuck's ranch to fish, but there are a dozen other ponds within easy driving distance of Bozeman that will give you a shot at some real lunkers. Again, these trips need to be planned well in advance through an outfitter. If you use Bozeman as a base of operations, your trout-fishing opportunities are almost unlimited.

Releasing a 10-pound rainbow in a Montana pond means you can catch it again.

Alan Gadoury works a small creek in Big Sky. You don't need big water to have fun.

The tailwater below the Glen Canyon Dam is more like a spring creek than the Colorado River . . .

There is just one other place that I really need to mention: **Lee's Ferry, Arizona**. In northern Arizona, the Glen Canyon Dam forms Lake Powell on one side and a tailwater for the Colorado River on the other. The only place to cross the Colorado and the Grand Canyon is at Lee's Ferry. Today, all the rafting trips for the Grand Canyon launch there and head downstream—the trout fisherman simply head upstream. What makes it such a special place

. . . and it can provide some monster rainbows and browns.

is that you are fishing in a crystal-clear trout stream often inches deep—at the bottom of the Grand Canyon. The scenery is spectacular.

Terry and Wendy Gunn operate Lee's Ferry Anglers in Marble Canyon, Arizona, which is about a four-hour drive north of Phoenix. They have a good number of excellent guides on staff, and a typical day will have you running upriver in a custom, shallow-draft riverboat to the base of the Glen Canyon Dam, then leisurely fishing your way back. The flies at Lee's Ferry are unique, if not outright strange— ginger scuds, Oregon Cheese Globugs, black/silver Zebra Midges, and a goofy orange Terry Gunn creation that imi-

Size 20 and 22 nymphs and 7X tippets are the rule at Lee's Ferry.

A collection of Lee's Ferry flies.

Terry points out a feeding trout to John.

tates a dead something—all on size 20 hooks. As in most areas, local fly patterns are best purchased at the Lee's Ferry Anglers Fly Shop. Most of the fishing will be sight-fishing from sandbars or shorelines, but very often drifting and casting streamers is the ticket. The river flow varies between 5,000 and 20,000 cubic feet per second, which stirs up lots of food, and the fish feed and grow like crazy. A room at

John Huarte fights a nice fish in the Glen Canyon.

A colorful Lee's Ferry rainbow holding in the current.

the Cliff Dwellers Lodge is only $65.00 a night, which is one of the last bargains left on earth.

November through February is spawning season, which provides the opportunity to sight-cast to large trout with egg patterns in addition to the usual midge fishing. March to May the weather warms, and as the spawning fish decrease, the nymphing action in the traditional riffles and runs increases. June through August brings the heat. The spawn is over, so you can plan on sight-casting dry flies to feeding fish and nymph fishing the runs. Since the Glen Canyon Dam controls the water flow, the warm nights and hot days have no effect on the fish—the water temperature stays in the 46- to 48-degree range year-round. In September, the air temperature drops back to a civilized level, but the dry-fly fishing continues until October, when the early

A nice rainbow caught on a Zebra Midge.

A 21-inch rainbow in spawning colors. TERRY GUNN

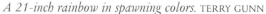

It took two strands of 7X tippet and a size 22 nymph to catch this guy.

The scenery in Marble Canyon is as impressive as the fishing.

Anglers are dwarfed by the canyon wall and amazed at the quality of the fishing at Lee's Ferry.

spawners move into the shallows. On any day of the year, an angler can land several dozen fat rainbows and browns between 15 and 22 inches. The enormous amount of insect life, scuds, and other food cause an extremely rapid growth rate, and every trout you'll catch will be fat, colorful, and healthy, if not very happy. A 2- to 4-weight rod is best for the dries and midges, and a 5- or 6-weight is better for the heavy nymphing or streamer fishing. The angling here is surprisingly more like fishing the spring creeks than a large river.

The best experience of fishing with Lee's Ferry Anglers is not really the fish at all. The trout are exceptional, but the scenery is breathtaking. Everywhere you look there will be massive rock monoliths, delicate arches, and mazes of canyons. You will find yourself looking up at 1,000-foot sandstone cliffs that haven't changed in centuries. Finding 365 days of spring-creek/tailwater fishing like this in the middle of the Arizona desert is truly amazing. It is a trip everyone should experience.

Alan Gadoury can be reached at (406) 586-3806 and algadoury@gomontana.com. His website is 6Xoutfitters.com. Contact Dan Bailey's Fly Shop in Livingston (DanBailey.com), the Rivers Edge in Bozeman (TheRiversEdge.com), Gallatin River Guides in Big Sky (MontanaFlyFishing.com), or Bozeman's Montana Troutfitters (troutfitters.com) to arrange a complete Montana vacation.

Lee's Ferry Anglers is on the web at Leesferry.com, or you can call Wendy Gunn toll-free at (800) 962-9755.

Salmon, Rainbow Trout, Arctic Char, and Grayling

PAT FORD

The gorge on the Newhalen River in Iliamna, Alaska.

An arctic char in spawning colors in September.

Silver salmon's noses aren't as weird as sockeyes', but they're close.

There is nothing like Alaska, especially in September. The air is crisp, the leaves are changing colors, the mountains are capped with fresh snow, and the fish are everywhere. The coastal streams are stacked full of spunky silver salmon that attack flies with abandon, even poppers chugged across the surface. Bright red sockeyes infest the inland streams, dumping millions of eggs between spawning and dying. Char, decked out in magnificent fall colors, follow the sockeyes feasting on eggs. Grayling are everywhere and never seem to lose interest in dry flies. Stream-born leopard rainbows take on a brilliant red centerline while trophy rainbows enter the streams feeding Lake Iliamna to fatten themselves up on eggs and salmon carcasses before winter's ice sets in. Everything in Alaska is vibrant in September—a magical place that is easily a fisherman's dream come true. If you long to catch a 30-inch rainbow, September in Alaska is the place to be, but planning such a trip is far from easy.

Between June and late September, there really isn't a bad time to fish Alaska, and the variety of fishing is overwhelming at times. When I began to organize my first trip, I was simply amazed at the lack of clear information available to help guide an angler through the thicket. Now, some fifteen trips later, I have tried almost everything that majestic state has to offer. If you are considering a fishing vacation in Alaska, here are some tips that might help.

The first question you must face is basic: What do I want to do in Alaska? So many attractive choices exist, it's best to start by eliminating some options. I can tell you how I made my cuts, but your decisions might be different.

Silvers are the most acrobatic and aggressive of all the Alaskan salmons.
BOB STEARNS

Spawning colors in September change almost daily.

I am not a rugged, backwoods type who likes roughing it, so that eliminated all of the tent-camping float trips at the get-go. I knew I wanted to fish exclusively with a fly rod, which eliminated the operations that touted deep jigging for giant halibut or downrigger trolling in salt water for king salmon. I don't like fishing in crowds, so the famed Kenai River failed to make the cut. After a few more rounds of dropping from consideration the lodges and camps and outfitters that offered experiences I could live without, I discovered I had "chosen" the Iliamna-Katmai area. That part of Alaska seemed to offer the fly fishing I wanted, and was easily accessible through Anchorage. Dozens of fishing lodges operate in this vast region, and each offers something unique. But they can be lumped into two general categories.

Fly-out lodges. Usually among the most expensive operations, most (but not all) fly-out lodges have pretty good fishing nearby for days when weather grounds the planes. This is an important consideration, Alaska weather being what it is. Weather permitting, upward of 90 percent of your fishing will be in remote waters you will be flown to for the particular fish you have elected to pursue. The lodge operators keep pretty good track of which rivers are hot, so they can usually put you on productive waters. You won't often be flown out to slow fishing.

Be sure to find out how and where you will fish when the planes can't fly and what the fishing is usually like at those fall-back spots. Many fly-out lodges have outstanding local fishing. The gorge at Rainbow King Lodge in Iliamna is probably the best sockeye hole in the world and is only a short truck ride away. You don't want to waste the "no-fly" days.

River lodges. Typically located on highly productive streams, river lodges and camps fish only one river system. These operations are favored by anglers who don't like flying around a foggy wilderness in small planes. Because

Kings are the first to arrive and are by far the biggest of the five salmons. BOB STEARNS

Catching silvers on poppers gives a whole new dimension to the fishing.

Battle Creek in September holds hundreds of spawning sockeye and rainbows.

river lodges don't have to pay for planes, pilots, and aviation fuel, they usually cost less than fly-out lodges. (If cost is a major consideration, be sure you find out how many extra airfares might be required to reach the camp, and don't forget to take tipping into consideration. These extras sometimes eat up a lot of the apparent savings.)

A river full of spawning sockeyes is quite a sight. TERRY GUNN

Rainbows fresh out of Lake Iliamna are almost completely silver. Actually, they are freshwater steelhead.

Some river camps and lodges provide one or two fly-outs in a weeklong package (usually at a hefty extra charge), but the majority of your fishing will be on the home river.

The lower price tag comes with its own price. No matter how good the river usually is, it had better be fishing well when you are there, or you are in for a long, frustrating week. Salmon runs are to some degree fairly predictable, but what you've heard about a certain week at one lodge doesn't necessarily apply to a nearby lodge on an adjacent river or even the same one. Pick your dates carefully and shoot for a week that usually coincides with the peak runs. Before you commit, ask about the history of high and low water problems on the river and what you can reasonably expect to catch if the salmon run of your choice shows up too early or too late or if water conditions are too high or too low.

Both fly-out and river operations run the gamut from very rustic to quite opulent. Choosing the right spot on that continuum of creature comforts is so much a matter of taste, lifestyle, and personality; I won't even try to give you any guidelines. I can say that if the accommodations are too basic, female guests will need to have a sense of humor. Guys are usually pretty flexible.

Some fishing lodges in both categories cater only to fly fishers, while others also accommodate spin fishers, trollers, and bait fishermen. If you are interested only in fly fishing, your best bet is a lodge that only takes fly-fishing clients. One of the others might be okay, but make sure they can provide the fishing you want. Ask a lot of questions and don't accept vague answers.

Sockeyes don't look much like salmon during spawn . . .

. . . in fact, they look more like monsters than fish.

Craig Augustynovich shows off a spawning silver salmon.

Pink salmon are small but a lot of fun on a 6-weight rod.
BOB STEARNS

Tom Robinson checks out the falls at Northeast Creek, one of Rainbow King's private leases.

If you can't get definitive answers to your questions from the booking agent or lodge manager, ask for the telephone numbers of previous clients—preferably ones who fished the same time the year before.

Over the years, I have become a regular at Rainbow King Lodge in Iliamna. It is a five-star hotel with planes, and it is located in the heart of the best rainbow trout fishing in the world. It's a very special place that I highly recommend. But there are other great lodges too.

Fish for the asking: Once you have selected where to go, your next decision is when, and that depends on what you want to catch.

Kings (what Chinook are called in Alaska) are the earliest salmon to show up. They generally arrive in June and are plentiful through mid-July. The largest of the salmon, they can approach 50 pounds (80 in the Kenai River, which partly explains the crowds) and put up a great fight when they are fresh from the sea. For kings, you need at least a 10-weight rod and 150 to 200 yards of backing and a full sinking line. Kings are hard to catch on a fly rod, and most are caught on lures or bait, often while back-trolling. Most fly-out lodges can provide both types of fishing.

Sockeye or red salmon are the next to appear. They enter fresh water in late June and peak around the Fourth of July. In most areas, the sockeye run fishes well through the end of July. Good fighters, sockeyes will jump repeatedly when they are silvery fresh from the sea. Although they don't eat during their spawning run, sockeyes will usually strike out of anger when an absurdly bright fly is dragged by their noses. The runs are so densely packed, you will probably snag more fish than will take your fly. It's possible to catch a hundred sockeyes per day, if that is your thing. Later in the season, the spawned-out sockeyes don't put up much fight and are inedible, but they do photograph well and make impressive mounts with their red bodies, green heads, humped backs, and hooked jaws.

Chum salmon show up in late July and run though mid-August. At 10 to 13 pounds average, they are a bit bigger than sockeyes and are almost as unusually colored. Soon after entering fresh water, chums develop hooked jaws and calico coloring. They take bright flies readily and are best fished in tidal creeks. They deteriorate rapidly in fresh water, and their food value is pretty low. There's a reason they are called "dog" salmon—native Alaskans only feed them to their dogs.

Pink salmon, the smallest of the lot, average about 5 pounds and only migrate heavily in even-numbered years. (In odd-numbered years, a few can usually be found mixed in with the chums.) Pinks hit flies avidly, fight well on a light fly rod, and are excellent table fare. After they have been in fresh water awhile, males develop an exaggerated hump—thus their other name, humpback salmon or humpies.

Silvers (coho salmon) are the last to arrive, usually in mid-August, and hang around through September. Averaging between 10 and 20 pounds, they are not as big as kings, but they take flies a lot more readily. They also fight hard, jump well, and taste great.

A leopard rainbow in spawning colors.

Grayling never lose interest in dry flies.

As the dead sockeye carcasses and eggs pile up, the rainbows leave the lakes and enter the streams to feed.

It's easy to see why plastic beads are the fly of choice.

Mike Waters with a 30-inch rainbow from the Rock Hole on the Lower Talarik.

Ready to go back to the lodge after a day on the Lower Talarik.

Rainbow trout, Arctic char, and grayling are available all summer long in most streams. Rainbows move out of the lakes into rivers early in June, which is the time to fish for them with dry flies. If an outfitter or operator promises dry-fly fishing after the Fourth of July, give him the third degree. As soon as the salmon runs begin, rainbows forsake insects and feed heavily on salmon eggs. So do char. The fishing can be pretty hot by normal standards, but in Alaska fly-fishing for rainbows in July and August is usually called "average." And you do have to work pretty hard for the big ones—those over 26 inches.

If your goal is a 30-inch rainbow trout, September is the time to fish. Monster fish—10 pounds and heavier—move out of the lakes to fatten up for the winter on eggs and rotting salmon carcasses. Fly fishing for giant rainbow trout is far and away my favorite pastime in Alaska. When you can catch trout up to 34 inches and 18 pounds, you know you are doing something really special.

Tackle. Unless you are determined to fish for gigantic king salmon, you don't need really heavy tackle for Alaska. My favorite salmon outfit is a 9-foot, 7-weight, 4-piece rod paired with a reel that will hold 150 yards of backing and a floating, weight-forward fly line. I use the floating line for pollywogs or poppers and a Teeny 200 for most everything else. I switch back and forth between these lines according to the fishing conditions. This outfit also handles trophy rainbows very well, especially when it gets windy. All you will need for trout is a 5- or 6-weight, and a 3- or 4-weight is great for dry-fly fishing for grayling. Don't bring just one rod to Alaska. All that climbing into and out of bush planes can be tough on tackle. I hadn't broken a rod in ten years, but I managed to

A coastal stream at low tide traps the salmon for the convenience of the brown bears and the anglers. The trick is landing the plane.

break three of them in four days on my first trip. Here is the minimum: a 5-weight for trout, a 7-weight for salmon and giant rainbows, and at least one 6-weight as a spare.

Flies. Whole books have been devoted to Alaska's fly patterns. There are hundreds of patterns for salmon—most are brightly colored and weighted. Big bead eyes also seem to help. Salmon are a fly tier's dream—most anything you come up with will work! Each lodge will have its own favorites and will either provide them on-site or be glad to send you a sample or two. The primary fly for trophy rainbows is not really a fly at all—it's a plastic bead. Years ago, I fought the bead fetish, but I eventually gave up . . . the beads simply work better than anything else and the surge of a 10-pound rainbow on a 6-weight rod will flush the "purist" out of anyone. In today's Alaska, beads rule. Egg-sucking leaches and flesh flies are pretty much backups, but they still produce fish.

My favorite silver salmon flies. Notice the ice—dress warmly in September.

A confrontation between an old and a young bear is actually pretty rare, since young bears do not appreciate getting pulverized. In September, the Kulik River has more bears than fishers.

Clothing. Lodge dress is pretty casual—jeans and flannel shirts do fine for dinner. However, most of your waking hours will be spent in chest waders, and Alaska's weather can change from 40 degrees and rain to 70 degrees and sun in what seems like minutes. Your objective is to stay warm and dry, so leave the lodge each morning prepared for the worst. Bring clothing that you can wear in layers. You will need polypropylene long underwear, some turtlenecks, a polar-weight polyfleece sweater, a nylon wind shirt, and the best rain jacket you can afford. Wearing all those layers, you should be able to tolerate the worst that Mother Nature can throw at you. It is a lot easier to take clothes off than to need an extra layer that you don't have with you. A small backpack is perfect for carrying extra clothes, tackle, and cameras and is highly recommended.

Quality fly-out lodges like Rainbow King on the shores of Lake Iliamna will let you pick your fishing each day. Do you want to fly to the coast for silver salmon?

The coastal brown bears often exceed 1,000 pounds in September.

Catch char or grayling? Rainbows? Do you want a shot at a 30-incher, or do you want to catch a bunch of 18- to 24-inchers? Do you like your rainbows with or without brown bears? Such decisions are very difficult to make day in and day out, but the biggest thrill I get on these trips is watching the bears feed on the spawning sockeyes. Sockeyes enter different stream systems at different times, but by late August, the spawn is in full bloom and candy-apple red sockeyes fill the streams. The rainbows, big and small, lie downstream of the "reds," feeding on the eggs, and the bears casually meander the shoreline feeding on the dead and dying salmon. They present no danger to anglers unless you ignore your guide's instructions and do something foolish like try to feed one a salmon. For me,

A sow and her cubs need to be watched carefully; they certainly will be watching you.

A perfect Alaska morning—days like this are made in heaven.
TERRY GUNN

No matter how cold it gets in September, the bears spend a lot of their time sitting in the river catching sockeyes.

they are what makes Alaska so very special. Don't ever pass up a trip to Brooks Falls in July or to Kulik River in September, and by all means bring a telephoto lens for your camera. Nature doesn't get any more amazing than it is on a cold September morning on a river full of bears. It is my absolute favorite way to spend a day in Alaska.

No matter when you go or which lodge you choose, fishing Alaska is expensive, but you don't want to visit a lodge that saves money by cutting down on the maintenance of its float planes. Yes, it is more crowded today than it was ten years ago, but so is everything else. Still, if you plan your trip carefully and make the choices that are right for you (which are not necessarily the ones I made), this will be one fishing trip you will never forget and will never match anywhere else in the world. Can you imagine tiring of catching big, strong, beautiful fish? In Alaska, it's possible. And perhaps only in Alaska. Contact Rainbow King Lodge at (800) 458-6539 or your favorite fishing travel agent.

Tuna and Wahoo

PAT FORD

Bermuda has the luxury of being entirely surrounded by fish.
BERMUDA'S DEPARTMENT OF TOURISM

Pastel colors abound in Bermuda.

The Fairmont Princess caters to anglers.

St. David's Light shows off the beauty of Bermuda's landscapes. BERMUDA'S DEPARTMENT OF TOURISM

About 600 miles due east of the Carolinas lies a fantastic cluster of islands known as Bermuda. Once the prime destination for spring break, Bermuda is still famous for its turquoise waters, pink beaches, and pastel houses, but what most people don't know is that there is no better place to catch a yellowfin tuna or wahoo on a fly.

What makes Bermuda unique is that about 25 miles off its southern coast, Argus Bank rises out of 2,000 feet of water to a depth of less than 200 feet. The currents that strike this undersea plateau create an upswell that pushes bait out of the depths toward the surface. The pods of bait in turn attract hoards of tuna and wahoo that can be chummed to the surface and into range of a fly rod.

The technique is quite simple: Boats anchor up on the edge of the Argus or Challenger Banks in a little over 200 feet of water. Hogmouth fry (known as glass minnows in Florida) make up the bulk of the chum, along with chunks of marlin or bonito. A steady stream of food is created as the current sweeps the chum into the depths. If all goes as planned, it won't be too long before various baitfish, little tunny, rainbow runners, and local seabirds known as shearwaters appear behind the boat. This commotion actually helps entice the tuna and wahoo out of the depths. On a good day, it's not unusual to have over twenty yellowfin tuna and a half dozen wahoo within 30 feet of the stern of the boat. At this point, the little tunny, rainbow runners, and the free-diving shearwaters become more of a liability than a help. The whole scene resembles a giant aquarium.

This 32-pound wahoo was my first on a fly.

Chumming Argus and Challenger Banks is most effective from late May through July and then again in September and October. Obviously, this style of fishing is most enjoyable in calm seas, so the summer months combine nice weather with water temperatures that the tuna prefer. In July and August, there are several tournaments that keep everyone busy, and it's also the best time for huge blue marlin. The marlin fishing in Bermuda is fantastic. The island record of 1,352 pounds was caught in 1995, and Captain Alan Card has personally boated six marlin over 1,100 pounds. However, there are actually more wahoo around in September and October, and after Labor Day, the charter boat captains are literally begging for business. The only drawback to early fall is that the weather can be a bit unsettled due to those pesty hurricanes that bounce off Florida and head north. Neverthe-

Fish aren't the only creatures that respond to chumming and chunking.

Captain Alan Card and Craig Reagor show off Craig's world-record amaco jack.

A light wire leader is a must to offset a wahoo's teeth.

Shearwaters can dive to 60 feet for free food.

Mike Muscatello, John Havlicek, and Bob Cheers show off a typical day's catch on Argus Bank.

less, if you have a few calm days in September, the fishing can be fantastic.

Yellowfin tuna are arguably the toughest fish you can target on a fly rod, and wahoo are probably the fastest. Both have exceptional eyesight, and a 40-pound fluorocarbon shock is necessary for the tuna, as is very light piano wire for the wahoo. If you use a standard wire leader, you'll be ready for wahoo, but you'll never get a tuna bite. In fact, you will rarely even get a wahoo bite. Time and again, we watched both tuna and wahoo swim right up to a fly on wire only to pass it by for the fluorocarbon leader. There is literally no hope of landing a wahoo on a monofilament leader, but, during my last trip, Flip Pallot convinced me to try the new titanium knottable wire in 20-pound strength, which led to my first wahoo on fly. The titanium is very thin and easy to use and, evidently, not overly visible. The best plan is to have a spare rod rigged and ready with the titanium wire for wahoo while you fish for the tuna, but after fighting a few of those brutes, you might decide to put the wire on just for the rest.

Bermuda's yellowfins can range from 20 to 100 pounds. The Bermuda records are 67 pounds on 12-pound tippet and 81 pounds on 15-pound. Unless you are chasing a specific record, there is little sense in using anything less than 20-pound test for your class tippet. These fish are all muscle and speed, and it's not unusual for a hefty yellowfin or wahoo to burn off 400 yards of backing on its first run. Sturdy tackle is a must if you want to have any hope of landing these creatures.

Since there is little need to cast more than 20 feet on Argus Bank, there is no need for a fly line longer than 30 feet. I've had the most success with a clear intermediate shooting taper. I actually dug out my oldest monocore tar-

pon line and cut it into 30-foot sections. Even the running line section was sufficient to flop the chum fly into the water, but I mostly used the weight-forward section, which allowed the semblance of casting. The short, thin fly line is a great advantage in fighting the fish, since it eliminates the "belly" created by dragging a 90-foot fly line through the water. At times, a floating line worked when the tuna were busting on the surface, as did a 400-grain sinking line when things were slow and the fish hung deep, but the clear intermediate shooting taper was best 90 percent of the time.

Large-capacity reels and 14-weight rods are a necessity for big yellowfins.

As with sailfish, I follow the shooting taper with 100 to 150 feet of 60-pound high-visibility monofilament, which puts a little stretch into the equation and provides tippet insurance. The rest of the spool is filled with backing—lots of backing. The Tibor Pacific is by far the most popular tuna reel, but my Nautilus 12-S also did a fine job. The best combination is a large-capacity reel with a perfect drag system matched with a fly rod with maximum lifting power.

Ian Card holds up a nice tuna for Bob Brien.

You really need a 15-weight fly rod for fighting tuna in over 1,000 feet of water. You can get by with a 12-weight if you insist on using lighter tippets, but you do not want to hook a 50-pound yellowfin on a 10-weight. Your rod, reel, and line should be geared to fight some of the strongest fish in the ocean in a place where they can go 300

Captain Steve Cabral displays a 50-pound yellowfin for Esteban Neely after a two-hour fight.

It's easy to match the chunks with sculpin wool flies.

A steady stream of chum is the ticket to bringing the tuna and wahoo to the boat.

yards straight down. Your job is to pump them back up 6 inches at a time. Your fly rod really can't be too heavy.

The fly selection for this chumming/chunking fishing is pretty unique. Most of the chum is hogmouth fry, which look exactly like a fly called a Gummy Minnow. The problem is that most of the Gummy Minnows on sale in fly shops are on light wire hooks. Blaine Chocklett (540-563-1617) ties this jelly-like fly on heavy-duty saltwater hooks. Most anything that appears in the chum line will eat Blaine's creation, including the birds.

The other ingredient in the chum is a chunk of marlin or bonito or any other dead fish that is handy, such as pilchers, robins (a.k.a. speedos), ballyhoo, or flying fish. The chunks vary in size, and the meat varies in color from light tan to dark red. Most flies collapse when they get wet or undulate in the current; chunks don't do either, so you need a fly that will hold its shape when it gets wet. Everyone who has tried fly fishing when "chunking" has faced this problem, but several years ago, Bob Brien found that spun sculpin wool held its shape underwater and matched the "chunk hatch" perfectly. It also could be trimmed to size on the boat if necessary. The end result looks like a giant glow-bug and was appropriately named the Bad Hair Day fly by Jeffrey Cardenas. I tie my own, but they can be ordered from Ben Walters at (423) 928-2007. I caught my wahoo and most of my tuna on this furball, and Flip had an 80-pound tuna nail it right on the surface before it even got wet enough to sink.

Taking a rest on Challenger Bank.

While you're fishing, there's plenty for the rest of your family to enjoy in Bermuda. BERMUDA'S DEPARTMENT OF TOURISM

Those are basically the only two style flies you need in Bermuda, but I'm sure any small deceiver fly on a stout hook would work. There is very little need to strip the fly at all—just letting it float back with the chum is most effective. Most of the time, the strike will occur in plain sight, 10 feet past your rod trip. You actually don't need a great number of flies or leaders each day, because after you fight two or three yellowfins, you're perfectly content to watch the show for the rest of the day. It's not unusual to spend over an hour on a 40-pound-plus tuna even on a 15-weight outfit. As an aside, there are no fly shops in Bermuda, so bring everything you conceivably may need, including a lightweight rainsuit.

Accommodations in Bermuda are never a problem. There are many five-star hotels, such as the Fairmont Hamilton Princess where we stayed as well as more economical establishments that still provide everything required by someone on a fishing vacation. Those who don't fish, however, will probably prefer the Princess and the dozens of excellent restaurants in the area. Hotel information can be obtained through the Department of Tourism Bermuda tourism.com or Fairmont.com. Captain Alan Card can be reached at AJCARD@northrock.bm, Captain Kevin Winter at PLAYMATE@lbl.bm, and Captain Steve Cabal at Bermuda sportfishing@hotmail.com.

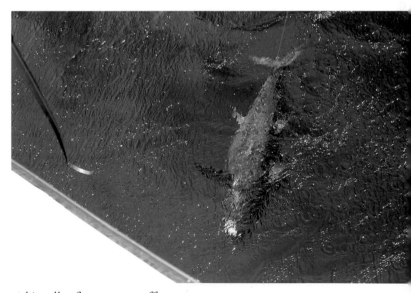

A big yellowfin comes to gaff.

Billfish

BILLY PATE

Fly-fishing for billfish is possibly the biggest thrill in fly fishing, just because it is extremely visible. Billfish "light up" when excited, and when one is teased into casting range in clear blue water and calm seas, the situation is so breathtaking you can almost forget to cast. There are many different ways to catch a billfish on a fly, and it can be done almost everywhere billfish are found, but your best chance for success today is in Guatemala or Costa Rica. Catching a billfish on fly is a team effort, but there is a lot the angler can do to contribute to his own success. If you want to catch a billfish on a fly, here are the techniques that have always worked for me.

If you have not caught a billfish on a fly, you need to start with Pacific sailfish. They are much bigger than their Atlantic cousins, averaging 80 pounds, and appreciably dumber, which is a good thing. The Pacific sails are very aggressive, tease up easier, and stay interested longer. A Pacific will stay behind the boat for several casts and will strike a fly repeatedly, unlike an Atlantic sail or white marlin that gives you one shot before it loses interest. After you have caught all the Pacific and Atlantic sails and white marlin you can stand, you can move on to the blues, blacks, and striped marlins. The technique for all these beautiful creatures is the same; it's just the success rate that drops out of sight when you move into the marlin arena.

I use a 12- to 14-weight rod for sailfish and even heavier for marlin. There are a number of excellent bill-

Teasing sailfish to the boat assures that the strike and the first set of jumps will be right behind the boat.

Using tube flies allows the fly to slide up the leader during the fight, but you have to hope nothing else eats it.

Do you think we have enough rods?

A good view of the tube fly and popper head.

fish rods on the market today—all with the power to control big flies and big fish. I like to have a fighting grip above the casting grip, which gives you more leverage and control, and it helps to have a butt piece that will fit securely into a fighting belt. These rods are designed for fighting fish, not for casting, since you will rarely need to get the fly more than 30 feet behind the boat. You need a short, shooting taper–style line in the 700-grain or above range. I use a fast-sinking 700-grain shooting taper so the fly will go underwater quickly and be more visible to the fish. I have had a better hookup ratio on sinking flies as opposed to poppers. The high-density 30-foot shooting taper also has very little drag in the water, as does a running line of a high-visibility monofilament in the 30- or 50-pound class. The monofilament gives you some stretch to help reduce pressure on the tippet when the fish runs fast, circles, or jumps. If you try to use a regular floating fly line, you will have problems.

A 30-foot shooting taper followed by 50 yards of monofilament covers your casting and line-drag hurdles, and again you want the smallest-diameter backing to reduce friction as the fish runs through the water. The new synthetic spectra-type braids in 50- or 80-pound test are excellent and come in chartreuse or hot orange so that boat captains can keep an eye on them from the bridge. When your sail begins to circle, there will be less pressure on the leader if the captain can follow the line rather than cutting directly to the fish.

The next area of importance is your reel. It has to have a smooth, steady drag and hold 500 yards of backing. Very rarely will you need that much, but you have to be

This fish tailwalked right to the back of the boat and then jumped into the cockpit, which livened things up considerably.

As the fight draws to an end, the sail usually turns a dark brown color. The Pacific sail is one of the most exciting fish to catch on a fly rod.

ready in case a marlin suddenly pops up instead of a sail-fish. No one I know has ever complained about having too much backing. I am partial to the Billy Page Marlin model reel in the anti-reverse style. I know Pat Ford favors the Tibor Pacific in direct drive. I like to reel with my left hand and use my strong arm for the rod. Stu Apte likes to reel with his dominant hand. It really doesn't matter which hand you use to reel in line—go with whichever you are used to—but be sure you have a reel that gains a substantial amount of line every time you turn the handle. Regaining 300 yards of line at 3 inches a turn is not fun.

Now for your leader. Attach 4 feet of 60-pound monofilament to the fly line with a double nail knot pulled together. The double nail knot is also the best knot to use between the fly line, monofilament running line, and the backing material. If you are going for a world record under International Game Fish Association rules, you must now tie a tippet to the front end of the 4-foot butt section. The monofilament tippet can have a breaking strength of 2-, 4-, 6-, 8-, 12-, 16-, or 20-pound test. Try to find a material that is very hard and abrasion resistant and very clear in color. The single strand of the class tippet must be at least 15 inches in length. It helps to double the tippet material on each end with a Bimini Twist, which will make the attachment knot stronger on each end. The final part of the leader, the shock tippet, should be made of 100-pound very clear mono. It can be no longer than 12 inches, including the knots on each end, which means that from the eye of the fly to the single strand of class tippet there can be no more than 12 inches. Tie one end to the double-line section of the tippet, and tie the other end to the hook of the fly. Unless you are

Randee Ward pulls on a sail in Guatemala.

A perfectly colored flying needle.

A sail's color changes continually during the fight.

A pork rind–enforced ballyhoo is the perfect teaser.

The perfect combo—a Tibor Pacific and Captain Ron Hamlin's fish fly.

really interested in a world record, use 20-pound Mason "hard"-type monofilament for your tippet.

Billfish flies have changed quite a bit over the years. Back in the old days, we didn't have the ultra-sharp hooks that we do today, and we thought the flies had to be huge. Today, we have synthetic fly-tying materials that don't retain water, can be adjusted to any length, and come in a rainbow of colors. When I caught my first billfish, no one had ever heard of a tube fly. Now, the most effective rig for hookup-to-strike ratios is a double rig of 5/0 Owner Octopus hooks behind a tube fly. Most boats you fish on will have their own fly favorites, and feathers still work well. Cam Sigler makes some of the best billfish flies on the market today, or you can call Captain Chris Dean at (305) 666-0908 for some custom flies that are the favorite in Guatemala.

Now for techniques. Fly fishing for billfish is necessarily a team effort composed of the angler, the boat captain, and the mate who teases the billfish within easy casting distance. The angler can then make a cast to a close, excited, and hungry fish. The mate's job is extremely important. If the sail is not teased effectively, it's not going to bite the fly . . . period.

I like to fish with two hookless teasing lines out. My fishing partner and I swap places between fly casting and retrieving the second teasing line—i.e., whichever line the billfish is not chasing—to get it out of the way. This happens at the same time the mate is working the line that holds the bait the billfish is chasing. The line that is retrieved can be held at the ready in case the other primary line is not productive for some reason, such as losing the bait to the fish, or the fish falls off the primary line and we want to search for it around the boat to get it hot on the teaser again.

The mate tries to bring the teaser bait to within 20 feet of the boat for the benefit of the caster. He should try to keep the fish about 3 feet behind the teaser as he reels it in closer to the boat. When he gets to within 20 feet, the mate may let the fish taste the bait for a moment. This is an important, yet risky, move, so the mate must have the rod low and pointed straight at the fish with no slack so he can jerk it away. As soon as the fish tastes the bait, the mate must immediately wind in the slack and throw the bait over his shoulder into the boat, getting it out of the billfish's sight.

As soon as he does this, the captain will take the boat out of gear, because to be eligible for an IGFA record and according to tournament rules, the boat must be out of gear before the angler casts the fly. Routinely, the captain will tell you when to cast.

The angler then makes the cast to a point about 5 or 6 feet to the side of and past the fish. If the angler is a right-hand caster, he will be on the right-hand side of the boat facing the stern, and the mate will be teasing from the left-hand side of the boat looking aft. The outrigger on the angler's side should have previously been raised so as not to interfere with the angler's backcast.

When the bait that the sail has barely tasted leaves the water, it thinks its prey has jumped and starts looking for it. When the fish sees the fly a bit behind its head and a bit to one side, it makes a turn and goes back for the fly. When he

Everything shakes on a sailfish.

In the air, sails are supreme contortionists.

Dolphin follow the Captain Hook by the hundreds.

A "lit up" sail at the end of a good fight. This photo is not computer colorized.

Every sailfish caught in Guatemala is released.

strikes "going away," there is a much better chance of hooking the fish in the comparatively soft flesh at the corner of its mouth. It is almost impossible to hook one coming straight at you, toward the boat, because the rims of the mouth behind and below the bill are bone and the hook won't penetrate enough to survive the first series of jumps.

When the fish is felt on the rod, the angler begins to strike and continues to do so until the fish jumps or makes a fast exit. When the captain sees you are striking the fish, he will put the boat in gear and move slowly forward in case the fish runs toward the boat. This enables the angler to keep his line tight while striking to drive in the hook.

When setting the hook, the angler should not raise the rod higher, but rather pull it back parallel to the water

Notice that the fish is hooked just behind the bill. Any farther out and it wouldn't have set.

Beach condos in Iztapa are not a good investment.

with the rod hand and pull the line in a foot or so with the other hand. The reason is if a person strikes and pulls up and the fish swims toward the boat, he can't pull in line effectively to keep it tight. Once you feel that the hook is set, just hang on and enjoy the ride. Hooking a 10-foot sailfish 30 feet behind the boat results in a spectacular series of jumps.

Whenever you see the sail coming up to jump, be ready to point the rod toward the fish and push it forward as he jumps. This is called "bowing." This reduces break-

But the sunsets are spectacular.

You will not find a more beautiful place than the Golfito Sailfish Rancho. STU APTE

Captain Ron Hamlin brings the Captain Hook *back home.*

ing pressure on the line since the fish's swimming speed increases to a much faster speed in the air because there is no more water resistance. Maintain your original pressure when he hits the water again, and don't increase your drag until you have the fish within 100 feet of the boat. Then you can increase it a couple of pounds, but be ready for another jump. When the fish is very close to the boat, the mate will reach for its bill and use pliers to get your fly hook free and back to you. After removing the hook, he may hold the fish by the bill while the captain moves slowly forward to revive it, and then release the fish alive and well. If you want a photo of the fish, tell the captain (and your cameraman) in advance, and the mate will pull it on board and hold it in front of you as you sit on the stern gunwhale. Be prepared to move quickly—the fish needs to go back to the water within a few seconds. There is really no reason to kill a billfish unless you are absolutely sure it will be a world record.

If you would like to see the things we have talked about in this chapter, but in exciting colorful action video with some extras, take a look at the videotape (or DVD) that was made when Jim and Kelly Watt joined me in the clear calm waters of Costa Rica a dozen years ago. It is called *Billy Pate's Fly Fishing for Billfish.* Jim and Kelly did some of the first ever underwater photos of billfish being teased and taking the fly in addition to all of the other action. You may reach them at FlyFishingVideos.com or email at info@Bennett-Watt.com.

There are a great many places that will give a shot at a sailfish on fly, but today your best bets are to contact Captain Ron Hamlin in Izapta, Guatemala, through South Fishing.com. Ron caught twenty-seven sails on fly in one day last year, and thirty to forty strikes a day are not uncommon. Anglers stay in a private, comfortable home with air-conditioning, satellite TV, and full meal service.

Another excellent choice and Stu Apte's favorite is Golfito Sailfish Rancho in Costa Rica. The lodge puts on numerous fly-fishing schools each year and operates a fleet of 27-foot Ocean Master boats that take out only two anglers each. In Guatemala, you are pretty much limited to sailfish, but at Golfito, you'll have shots at blue marlin, cubera snapper, and roosterfish, and you can also tour the nearby rain forest on the shores off the Golfo Dulce. It's an easy plane trip from Miami to San Jose after which the lodge will provide a shuttle flight to Golfito. The peak season for sailfish in Guatemala is December through May. More information can be obtained at GolfitoSailfishRancho.com or call (877) 726-2648.

Swordfish on Fly

PAT FORD

Perhaps the most impressive catch of a billfish on fly in Florida occurred in August 2003 when Marty Arostegui caught a swordfish on fly off Miami. Today, Marty holds more than 100 IGFA world records, but his best catch never made the hook—it was 1 inch too short to legally keep.

Marty's catch is the only swordfish to be taken on a fly in the United States, and it did not happen by accident. Marty joined with Captain Bouncer Smith and formed a plan. From past trips, they knew that green Hydro Glow lights placed in the water at night attract swordfish— sometimes. Marty decided to take his 14-weight fly rod matched with a large-capacity, large-arbor reel, and put on a heavy fast-sinking line to get the fly down. The fly itself was Marty's creation. It was a big, double-hook white fly with a small cylume light in the middle to give it the luminescent look of a squid.

Drifting in relatively calm seas in more than 1,000 feet of water, Marty would cast out about 80 feet of line and then patiently let it sink at least 40 feet. His retrieve consisted of short jerks and a long pause—much like the action of a squid. Each retrieve lasted more than five minutes if he did it right. Marty got his first bite about an hour into the trip. He set up hard, and he could feel something very heavy shaking its head, but the hook fell out.

Marty and Bouncer continued to drift north from Key Biscayne to Government Cut, flat lining two hookless baits and casting the heavy fly rod. An hour after the first bite, it happened again. This time the fish hit like an

Dr. Marty Arostegui holds up the first and only swordfish ever taken on fly in the United States. MARTY AROSTEGUI

express train and hooked itself just like a good fish is supposed to do. The first run left Marty in fear of being spooled, but the swordfish stopped, and Marty was sure it was a tuna or a foul-hooked shark until the 40-pound swordfish floated into the lights. The fish was 46 inches long and, after several photos, was released. It will be quite a while before that feat is repeated, but Marty proved it can be done, even in Miami.

Marty's swordfish flies are similar to every other billfish fly except that he attaches cylume "lunker light" to the midsection.

Peacock Bass

PAT FORD

Thankfully, River Plate's floating tent camps now have air-conditioning.

There are several species of peacock bass, but they actually aren't bass at all—they're cichlids. The most common variety is the butterfly, which is found in Florida and the Amazon. As far as anglers are concerned, the other International Game Fish Association (IGFA) species is the "speckled peacock," which grows to 30 pounds and comes in two color patterns. Biologists disagree whether the color patterns are actually different species, but in Brazil the "paca" has a brownish, gray color with white spots, and the "tucunare" or "barred" has a yellow color with three prominent black vertical bars. Evidently, these two color patterns interbreed, so IGFA keeps them as one species, but they are found in various blends of both color patterns. For our purposes, all you need to know is that the "grandes" are what you want to catch when you go to Brazil, and they are well worth the trip.

If you want to fly-fish for peacocks in Brazil, the most important factor to consider is the water level. The Amazonia peacocks season is roughly from September through March, and a lot depends on whether you are above or below the equator. You are fishing in the world's largest rain forest, and the key word is "rain." Even the tributary rivers can be 20 to 40 feet higher at the end of the rainy season than at the end of the dry season. When the water is high, it extends well into the jungle and so do the fish. Water levels vary with each watershed, and while one area may be having a flood, another can be suffering from a drought. When you are booking a trip, you cannot grill the travel agent or the lodge enough about the water levels. Every year is different, but do everything possible to fish during low water; the lower the better. You also want falling rather than rising water, so do as much research as possible before selecting a lodge and a time. Timing your trip is everything.

Butterfly peacock average around 4 pounds.

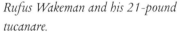

Rufus Wakeman and his 21-pound tucanare.

During high water, the creeks lead to lagoons full of fish.

Dr. Randee Ward shows off a "paca" or spotted peacock.
STEVE WARD

Water levels are far more important for fly fishermen than plug casters. With a few exceptions, the water being fished will be dark with limited visibility. If the fish are roaming around a flooded jungle, they are not going to come out of the trees for a streamer—they won't even know it's there. The plug fishermen throw giant lures called "wood choppers" and "rip rollers" that send up to 2 feet of spray with each jerk. It seems to me that the peacocks are attracted to the noise as much as anything else, and I have had some hit the plug so hard and fast that they knocked it 15 feet into the air. The strikes are what you would expect from an amberjack being teased with a blue runner. There really is nothing about these fish that resembles "bass." Cubera snapper would be a more accurate comparison. The way they hit those woodchoppers is fantastic, but when the water is low, anglers will actually get more fish on flies.

My first trip to the Amazon was a bit of a disaster. I was booked with an outfitter that pulled a series of sleep-aboard tent-barges upriver behind a small mother ship. The theory was that you could get to remote, low-water areas that even the live-aboards couldn't reach. I was part of a two-week program, and I reasoned that whatever the water level was the first week, it would be lower the second week. Well, the first week was a great success. Two of the guys were fishing fly, and they released 853 peacocks up to 16 pounds in six days. That level of excitement easily made up for the lack of air-conditioning in the tents. However, when my group stepped off the plane in Manaus, we were told that we were going to a different camp on a different river. Again, only two of us were fly fishing, and the explanation for the change was to provide "bigger fish." Well, we also got "bigger water." Fly fishing turned out to be an exercise in futility—we managed only a few butterflies each day— about one every hundred casts—until we finally gave up and picked up plug rods. I did catch an 18-pound paca on a rip-roller, but I was terribly disappointed in the fly fishing. Once again, whenever you book your trip, make sure there will be low water and no surprise changes.

There are a number of excellent lodges and houseboats in Amazonia, and a reputable agent such as Quest, Amazon Tours, South Fishing, or Sweetwater Travel will do their best to give you the trip of your life—just make it clear that you want to fly-fish. Most operations are not set up for fly fishing, and many of the guides do not understand that we do things differently than the plug casters. Insist on a guide that knows what a fly rod is, and get a firm commitment from the lodge when you book the trip. It is also important that you share the boat with another fly fisherman. If one guy is casting plugs, and the other is trying to fly-fish, there are going to be major problems. Most Amazon boats are 18 feet long, give or take a foot. All have electric motors that creep the boat along the shoreline, allowing the anglers to cast to pockets and structure. Well, the range of the plug rod is well over 100 feet, and a good fly caster will be throwing 60 feet on average. Distancing the boat from the

Piranha are a lot of fun, but keep your fingers away from their jaws.

During low water, the fish are still in the lagoons, but getting to them is not as easy. STEVE WARD

In the Amazon, even the minnows are nasty.

Releasing a peacock in the middle of a lagoon can prove fatal for the fish.

Most of the fishing in the Amazon requires casting to shorelines.

shoreline thus becomes a problem. It is a better plan to have the same type fishermen in a boat so that they can share the good water equally.

The Amazon River system is not a friendly place if you are a fish. Instead of bluegills, they have piranha. Everything that wasn't equipped with size, speed, poison stingers, or fangs has long since become extinct. Even the relatively toothless arawana amuses itself by leaping into tree branches and eating birds. With the possible exception of the several species of giant catfish and the reclusive pirarucu, the tucunare is the meanest fish in the place. It eats everything that it even thinks it can fit into its mouth. I personally watched a trio of 20-pound peacocks chase a school of butterflies right up onto the beach. We caught one of the group—while it was in the process of eating one of its 3-pound cousins—it weighed 24 pounds. While 2-inch Clousers may work fine in Miami, they don't in Brazil. Big fish want big food, but big food is often hard to cast on a fly rod.

Peacock flies are best made of synthetic materials—the tougher the better. You need a big wide profile but not a long one. If the fly is too long, you are going to miss a lot of short strikes from butterflies and other weird creatures that inhabit the region. Let's face it—catching strange-looking things that try to bite your fingers off is fun—just let the guide handle them. If your fly starts out too long, the piranha will quickly shorten it for you. There really isn't a need for a fly much more than 5 or 6 inches long, but it does have to sink quickly, so large, heavy hooks (3/0 or 4/0) are important, and they have to be very sharp. Fortunately, there are many fine tarpon hooks on the market that are perfect for peacock flies. If you can coat the head with

You never know what you're going to come up with in the Amazon.

epoxy, the fly will last a lot longer, and big eyes are a must. When you are finished, you have something that double-hauls just slightly more efficiently than a wet hamster. If you think a Merkin is hard to cast, wait until you try these things. Nevertheless, casting is a major part of peacock fishing, so some compromising is in order.

The answer to this dilemma is to design a fly pattern that is big enough to attract a 15-pound peacock, yet light enough for you to cast effectively. You want the biggest fly you can cast. Experimenting at home helps, and it is important to remember that a wide profile does not necessarily mean a thick, heavy fly. Try to use less rather than more materials. Combinations of green-yellow-orange and blue-white-red work exceptionally well. Again, add as much flash as possible, but remember, you will have to cast it over 60 feet about a thousand times a day. Don't get carried away with the materials. If you don't tie your own flies, Captain Chris Dean ties excellent peacock patterns and can be reached at (305) 666-0908.

Once you have found the right fly, you will need tackle that is heavy enough to cast it, yet light enough to be thrown constantly for ten hours a day. One year, I fished the Rio Negro Peacock Bass Fly Tournament, and by the time it was over, my fly casting was greatly improved, but I felt like a fiddler crab with blisters. Nevertheless, I can safely say that everyone in the tournament used a 10-weight rod with an intermediate sink line—tarpon taper monocores to be specific. The rod is very important, and while each angler had his favorite, we all used stiff, fast-action graphite rods and overloaded them with 11-weight lines. I carried a back-up 10-weight with a 10-weight monocore, but it had trouble handling the bigger flies, especially as the day wore on

I'm pretty sure we never got this fly back.

My favorite peacock bass patterns.

Wading the sandbars with an 8-weight produces fast action on butterflies.

Everything in the Amazon eats flies.

and I got tired. The heavier line is a big help in turning over the big flies, but the straight 10 was more fun when casting the smaller flies to the butterflies. Again, each angler should use what he is comfortable with, but I can promise you that on the big rivers a 9-weight is too light and an 11-weight is too heavy. The reel is less important. You need a good drag and about 100 yards of 30-pound or heavier backing, but try to keep the combo as light as possible.

The 10-weight rod also comes in handy fighting the bigger fish. Peacocks are not known for long runs. They smash flies with gusto, and then when they feel pressure, they simply look for the closest tree and head for it. The jungle is usually not far away if the water is high, and stopping that first run is a real problem, so bring a few spare rods just in case the fish wins. During my first trip, the water was very high, and most of our strikes were in the middle of a forest. I had fish straighten out 3X hooks, tear hooks right off the plugs, and two snapped 65-pound Power Pro. Now you see why I stress low water for fly fishing. Watching your $65 fly line disappear into the bushes is a painful experience, since it never comes out in quite the same condition that it went in. When the water is low, the trees are way up on the bank, on land, where they should be: separated from the water by a sandy beach. Low water makes all the difference.

There is a calmer side to all this. In low water, the sandbars form gullies and beaches. Schools of butterfly peacocks cruise the shallows like bonefish and are great fun on lighter rods and more civilized-sized flies. We spent at least an hour each day walking the shoreline, occasionally kicking alligators out of the way, and casting to butterflies, which, by the way, are probably the most beautiful fish I have ever seen. They are lime-green with black spots, yellow and orange trim, and iridescent blue fins. Believe me, you will really enjoy wading and sight-casting to 3- to 5-pound butterflies with a 7- or 8-weight outfit, especially toward the end of the week.

Once you have amassed about fifty castable flies and found a rod-and-line combination that you can use effectively, you needn't worry about tippet strengths—most people don't even use one. Peacocks are not leader-shy, and it is acceptable to simply use 5 or 6 feet of 40- or 50-pound test right from the fly line to the fly. IGFA rules are sacrificed for the fun of just catching fish and the probability of losing a big fish to the underbrush if you have a tippet. The plug casters use 65- or 80-pound Power Pro straight to the lure.

During my first trip, I lost a good number of fish by trying to pull them out of the structure. After half a dozen depressing encounters, one of the more experienced anglers took me aside and explained the situation: When they get in the trees, stop all pressure and the fish will stop. The guide will then motor over to the edge of the jungle, jump overboard into the snake- and piranha-infested waters, follow the line back into the bushes, and, if you are lucky, return with your fish. If you're not lucky, you will never see your fish, plug, Boga Grip, or guide again.

Now, try to imagine this scene with a fly rod and what will be left of your fly line. If you use a 20-pound tippet, the break-off will hopefully occur before your line is

A 10-weight rod and an intermediate sink line is the perfect combination for the Amazon.

During high water, the guide may have to earn his tip.

My 21-pound peacock bass taken on fly at the Rio Negro Lodge.

Mitch Widom shows off proper sun protection and an arawana.

completely destroyed. Having a few spare lines, rods, and everything else, is always a good idea on the Amazon. If you like poppers, bring a floating line, and it is always a safe bet to have a Teeny 300 just in case the fish are holding in the deeper pools. In my opinion, the monocore is the easiest to cast, which makes it my first choice.

If you really want to fly-fish and follow the rules, a 20-pound tippet of a hard mono, such as Mason, and a 50-pound shock are the way to go. If you are looking for records, don't cast near structure; work the beaches, gullies, and flats, and keep your eye out for bubbles. Tucunare are very protective of their young and guard them for weeks after birth. When danger threatens, the fry will actually hide in the parent's mouth. Every so often, the parents will take the school of babies out into open water and let them swim around at the surface, which creates a raindrops or "bubbles" effect on calm water. If you can spot one of these small patches of bubbles and get your fly into it, it will be instantly attacked by the parent. I caught my biggest fly fish, a 21-pounder, casting to bubbles. Since the fish was hooked in open water, I probably could have caught it on most any tippet. If you want a record, keep a rod rigged for bubbles, but don't waste your time throwing a 12-pound tippet near structures unless you have a whole lot of extra flies.

The most amazing record performance I know of was on the Itapara River by my friend Marty Arostegui. Marty has over 100 IGFA world records, many of which are for species of fish that I cannot even pronounce, much less identify. Marty is a 4-pound and 6-pound tippet master, and he always keeps one of these super-light rigs ready for peacocks, which I always considered a waste of time.

Marty Arostegui holds up his IGFA-record 15-pound peacock on 6-pound tippet. This is an unbelievable catch.

MARTY AROSTEGUI

It's always possible to make a long run upriver and do some real camping.
MARTY AROSTEGUI

Well, one day he found a lagoon with hardly any debris. He caught a 15-pound peacock on 6-pound test and a 14-pound peacock on 4-pound tippet. Both fish fought for over thirty minutes in open waters. You cannot imagine what an accomplishment this is on a fly rod.

The final question you must ask yourself before boarding a plane to Brazil is how do you react to heat? By heat, I mean "August in Islamorada bake-you-to-death heat." In the Amazon, you will be fishing right on the equator, and your outfitter will give you a good checklist for clothing—pay attention to it. It is extremely hot, humid, and often windless. I nearly died on my tent-camp experience. Most of the guys had no complaints, but I would have killed for an air-conditioned room and a hot shower. As I get older, I appreciate my creature comforts more and more. If you enjoy roughing it, then you will be fine anywhere, but many of the lodges are literally four-star hotels in the middle of the jungle, so you do have a choice of comfort levels. Finally, if you do find yourself bathing in the river, watch out for stingrays and the most feared fish in the Amazon: a tiny catfish that has a habit of entering the human body through the urinary orifice, where its spines prevent it from being removed without surgery. Personally, I never went into the water over my knees!

A serious tucunare from the Royal Amazon Lodge.

Peacock bass trips are universally one week in length, basically because there is only one flight to and from Miami and Manaus each week. There are any number of excellent lodges and mother ships in the Amazon, and all you need to do is contact an agent who will take care of all the travel details.

For more information on peacock bass fishing in Brazil, check out SouthFishing.com, Amazontours.com, RoyalAmazonLodge.com, Peacockbassassociation.com, AmazonVoyager.com, and Fishquest.com.

Golden Dorado

PAT FORD

Larry Dalberg shows off what we were promised: a 40-pound golden dorado, taken on fly.
STEVE YATOMI

No matter how careful you are or how well you prepare for a trip, some turn out to be disasters. Usually it's because of bad weather or unexpected water conditions, and those situations really can't be avoided. However, there are times when the adventure that is promised by the lodge or outfitter turns out to be a complete nightmare and, in retrospect, never really had a chance to be anything but a nightmare. Fortunately, if you manage to survive a trip from hell, you can usually look back and laugh at it—after a while. I've had more than my fair share of poor to rotten vacations, but quite possibly the worst was a trip to Argentina for golden dorado.

When I mention golden dorado, I'm talking about a sleek, toothy, bright yellow freshwater cousin of the tigerfish, not the blue/green saltwater dorado (a.k.a. dolphin). Argentina's dorado are the perfect predator—fast, acrobatic, and equipped with strong jaws and lots of sharp teeth. My research told me that the most common destination to catch them is the Ibera Marsh, but the fish there are relatively small, rarely weighing over 15 pounds. What I was looking for was a place to catch golden dorado over 20 pounds. Then one day I met an outfitter from Argentina who had just set up an operation in Miami. He was an extremely pleasant fellow who produced impressive photos of golden dorado in the 30-pound range, allegedly taken on fly in a

We knew we were in trouble before we ever got to the park.
JIM RIST

The Bermejo River was hyped as holding golden dorado and trout up to 7 pounds. What a joke! JIM RIST

Camping would have been more fun if it wasn't for the bugs, heat, and "banditos."

Rufus Wakeman changes flies before working a pool on the Tarija River.

clear river in a national park in Bolivia. This was exactly the situation I had dreamed of, so I corralled a few of my friends, and we set up a trip. The plan was to fly to Buenos Aires and then to a town in northwest Argentina, after which we would be driven to a lodge on the bank of the Bermejo River, which was described as a bit "reddish," but full of dorado and trout up to 6 or 7 pounds. We would fish there for a day and a half and then drive into Bolivia to cabins that the outfitter owned just outside a Bolivian national park. We would camp there and fish inside the park in the Rio Grande de Tarija River, which was promised as the only "crystal-clear stream that holds truly world-record dorado." Allegedly, the biggest fish from the prior season was over 43 pounds—at the time, the IGFA fly-rod record was actually around 10 pounds, so this size dorado was pretty exciting. The explanation for the huge size of the fish was that special permits were needed to enter the park, and it was hardly ever fished by anyone, much less a group of experienced Florida fly rodders such as ourselves. We were each promised multiple hookups each day with fish between 10 and 30 pounds.

Our first clue of the impending disaster was when we learned that we had actually been booked on different flights—two out of the five were on an earlier flight than we had been told. Fortunately, we discovered this on our own, barely in time for everyone to get on a plane head-

We all agreed that the river looked fishy—there just weren't any. JIM RIST

ing south. We made it to Buenos Aires and then to San Salvador de Jujuy, where we were driven by truck to the so-called lodge. The trip turned out to be closer to five hours than the two hours predicted, and on the way, the outfitter explained that the Bermejo River was washed out and unfishable so we would proceed directly to the park the next morning, where from all reports, the fishing had been spectacular. He also mentioned that there had been some "bandito" activity around his cabins, so we were going to camp in tents inside the park near the ranger station to avoid any unpleasantries, like kidnapping. Naturally, we all agreed that this was a good plan, since none of us wanted to be kidnapped, robbed, tortured, or shot. Fishermen are the ultimate optimists, and we all felt that camping would be fun—part of the adventure of "extreme dorado fly fishing" as the trip was promoted.

Well, the trip from the lodge to the park was amusing at best. We were all piled into two small Toyota trucks with our rods, luggage, camping supplies, and food dumped in the back. As we started out, our guide mentioned that we had to stop in a town on the way for a few minutes to pick up last-minute supplies and confirm that all our permits were in order. That short stop took three hours, but eventually we were bumping down a dry, dusty dirt road following flatbed trucks loaded with sugarcane on our way to the park entrance. We felt like we were in a convoy in Afghanistan.

After about two hours of dust, we finally reached the ranger station next to a rather picturesque river. It wasn't

The poverty of the natives made it clear why there were no fish outside of park waters. JIM RIST

We worked every inch of every pool without a bite. JIM RIST

Dr. Steve Ward shows off the only fly-caught dorado of the trip.

Hiking along the riverbank brought to mind broken ankles, falls, and snakes. JIM RIST

Lunch didn't exactly live up to its pre-trip description.

exactly crystal clear, but it was at least water that held a fish none of us had ever seen. We all hopped out of the truck with great enthusiasm, only to find out that the ranger wouldn't let us in the park—some problem with our permits or lack thereof. Hadn't our guide just spent two hours in some town just outside the park confirming our permits? Surely this misunderstanding could be cleared up with a phone call, so Rufus Wakeman handed our leader his satellite phone. Well, that didn't work either. After several hours of negotiations, we were told that we would have to camp on the riverbank outside the park while our outfitter's Bolivian partner went back to town to clear up this silly misunderstanding. Somehow, the "bandito" problem wasn't brought up as tents were pitched on a sandy beach along the river. We finally started fishing around 4 P.M.

That afternoon five world-class fly fishermen covered over a mile of the Tarija River without getting a bite from anything. We hit every hole, ripple, backwash, and rock without so much as spooking a fish of any species until it was too dark to see the water. Dinner consisted of some form of dead animal that tasted like a combination of underarm deodorant and rubber, and as it turned out, the refrigeration system consisted of a wooden box with two blocks of ice. The wine, however, was excellent.

The new plan was as follows: In the morning, we would be driven about 2 miles up the river and fish our way back to the camp in time for lunch. By that time, Jose should be back from town with the proper permits, and we could move into the park. The tent accommodations were actually quite comfortable, but the bugs were lethal.

I must admit that the river was interesting and looked fishy. The five of us covered every inch of that river, dropping flies in every pool and run that we came to as we trekked downstream toward camp. On trips like this, I always bring a plug or spin rod, if permissible, just for insurance. Dorado are known to hit big shinny plugs and spoons, and carrying an extra rod is usually worth the effort if it turns out to be the only way to catch a fish. During the first hour, Steve Ward actually caught a dorado around 7 pounds, and shortly thereafter, Rufus thought he had a strike from something but never saw it. Most of our time was spent trying to cross rapids without drowning or climbing along rock-strewn banks wondering what kind of snakes lived in Bolivia. Eventually out of frustration, I broke out the plug rod so I could cover more water faster, hoping at least to wake up whatever was there, but I never got a strike, nor did anyone else. We all managed to drag ourselves back to camp around 1:00 P.M., where the temperature in the lunch tent was 107 degrees. While we were eating cheese and Spam sandwiches, Jose showed up with a great story. Somehow, within 24 hours, the entire national park had been closed to fishing, and all permits had been revoked. At this point, our esteemed outfitter suggested that we could drive around to the back of the park and sneak into the river. Since I had little interest in spending the next few years in a Bolivian prison, that suggestion was firmly declined. The only alternative was to stay in camp and fish the public water. After a major meeting, we decided to fish the afternoon, spend the night, and then head home the next morning. We were not happy but that afternoon I did manage to catch two dorado on the plug rod—one fish was about 8 pounds, the other 13. The flies never got a bite. At least we got to see a golden dorado, and they are spectacular creatures. I can't imagine how much fun one in the 30-pound range would be on a fly rod. Everything said about the species was true—there just weren't any dorado to speak of in the water we had traveled a day and a half to fish.

I'm sure the sand fleas and no-see-ums were sad to see us leave, but we somehow made it back to the lodge, where we learned that the Bermejo River was actually unfishable due to some major construction upstream rather than a recent rainstorm, so there was no hope of catching anything there. We did, however, manage to change our flights and return to Buenos Aires and Miami and somehow got

The beach bugs were very unhappy to see Ted Rist leave.

Martin Carranza and Steve Ward show off two-thirds of the fish we caught in Bolivia.

This was the most activity we saw in the river in two days. JIM RIST

Ted Rist and Rufus Wakeman end the day and the trip totally frustrated. JIM RIST

As a species, the golden dorado is a prefect predator.

home with only a few thousand bug bites as our trophies. My good friend Captain Bill Curtis was bringing a group down for the same trip two weeks after ours, and at least I was able to convince our outfitter to take them somewhere else. Bill was seventy-nine years old at the time, and our experience would surely have killed him. As it turned out, Bill and his group were taken to different rivers and stayed in hotels with amenities such as food and hot showers. Bill actually caught an IGFA-record dorado, which made him pretty happy, but no one on either trip ever saw a dorado over 15 pounds, much less the 30-pound trophies we were promised. Fortunately, our outfitter is no longer offering this Tarija River package, but the truth is that we would have been perfectly happy to put up with the tents, bugs, and heat if we had each caught a 30-pound dorado. In the outfitters' defense, he thought he had all the permits and legal technicalities confirmed, and somewhere between Miami, Argentina, and Bolivia's national park service, our "extreme dorado fishing" wound up in our nightmares. We took a chance on the trip of a lifetime and lost, but those things happen. It was an adventure—it just wasn't a pleasant one. It did teach me that if you're the very first to fish a particular area, there's probably a reason no one has been there before. It always pays to talk directly to someone who made the same trip with your outfitter before putting down a deposit.

Several months later, I received an e-mail from Steven Yatomi of Adventure Travel Alliance, who was on the Uruguay River in Argentina with Larry Dahlberg filming an episode of *The Hunt for Big Fish.* He took great pleasure in telling me that they had found the place I had been searching for. One morning, Larry caught ten golden dorado over 40 pounds on lures and on flies, and during the course of the trip, Steve caught two that he was sure were over 50 pounds. These fish were literally too big for a Boga Grip, because of the probability that their immense body weight would dislocate their jaw during the weighing. Steve felt that these were truly trophy fish and that eventually every IGFA record for golden dorado would come from the Uruguay River.

When he got back, Steven explained that the fish are located in a tailwater below the Salto Grande Reservoir called La Zona. Evidently, the government just recently opened up this fishing in exchange for continuous management and conservation studies. Fishing is done from specially designed skiffs, and no one may fish more than four days in a row. This is a large body of water, so 10-weight rods and deep sinking lines are necessary. The flies cannot

A Boga Grip is the best way to handle any fish with powerful jaws.

be too big or too gaudy—the most effective lure evidently is a bright orange 18 Mag Rappala. Accommodations are provided at nearby lodges and hotels that provide comfortable rooms, excellent meals, swimming pools, experienced guides, and well-designed skiffs for fly casting.

We took a chance on our dorado expedition, but part of the adventure was that we were going to be among the first Americans to fish this area, and it was supposed to be sight-fishing instead of dredging—that is what sold us on the idea. Our experience simply reinforced my rule that you really must deal with an established, reputable outfitter or travel agent at all times. If you want to catch that 40-pound golden dorado, check out Larry Dahlberg's experience at HuntforBigFish.com and then contact Steven Yatomi at AdventureTravelAlliance.com, and don't forget to bring a plug or spinning rod just to speed up the action. A little extra insurance never hurts.

Larry Dahlberg shows off a golden dorado close to 50 pounds. The huge plug gives you an idea of the best size and color fly.
STEVE YATOMI

Sea-Run Brown Trout

PAT FORD

Tierra del Fuego means "land of fires." Today it also means giant brown trout.

No one goes to Tierra del Fuego for a weekend. It is at the very tip of South America and is the closest landmass to Antarctica. The scenery is nonexistent, and the temperature in February parallels Alaska in August. On a nice day, the wind blows at only 25 mph—40 mph is typical. Anglers go there to fish a river that comes in from the ocean and snakes its way through sheep ranches and grasslands into Chile. There is almost no native wildlife except a few ultra-fat beavers and a bunch of foxes. The fishing, however, is legendary.

Tierra del Fuego was named by Magellan in 1520 as the "land of fires" after seeing smoke from signal fires lit by the natives in response to sighting his tall ship. In the 1930s, British angling enthusiasts introduced the first brown trout to the Rio Grande River. How they managed to transport trout from Europe to this extremely remote region is beyond me, but the browns evidently took one look around the Rio Grande and headed for the ocean. What is very strange is that they return to the river to spawn each October through April, and every year the numbers and size of the fish have been increasing. Evidently, these fish have few natural predators. It is believed that up until 1960 fewer than two hundred fisherman had ever hooked a sea-run brown trout in the Rio Grande. Joe Brooks and A. J. McClane wrote about their visits in the

Bob Stearns shows off a dry-fly prize. BOB STEARNS

The scenery isn't much to look at. BOB STEARNS

Tom Robinson with a 30-pound brown.
TOM ROBINSON

A nice buck that's been in the river a while. CHICO FERNÁNDEZ

a ton of it. The quad-tip lines are a good system, but the sinking tips are relatively short. The problem with the short sinking-tip lines is that no matter how deep you get the fly, as soon as the floating line gets caught in the current or you start to retrieve, the fly goes up. Several anglers had spey rods that could lay out 100-foot casts like clockwork—if you knew how to use one—and the quad-tip lines seemed to work well for them. I ultimately found that a Teeny 200, 300, and 400 covered all the bases. During my ultra-high water trip, I probably could have used a 500 or a full-sink grade IV striper line that really drags the bottom. It's a lot better to bring extra lines than to get there and discover that the key to success is sitting on your fly table back in the states.

Leaders were usually kept above 10-pound test. These sea-run browns were not particularly leader shy and could reach more than 30 pounds. Anything under the 10-pound test is going to cost you a lot of flies and missed opportunities. I think the record for the Rio Grande is 49 pounds, and if you check the IGFA book, almost every fly-rod record for brown trout comes from Tierra del Fuego. This is no place for 4X tippets.

The next decision had to be which fly to use, which turned out to a problem. I readily admit that I am a total gear head, but when it comes to flies, I am completely out of control. I tie my own and use it as a form of relaxation—a form of "male knitting." Before I left, Larry Dahlberg told me that he'd had great success with extra big black flies. All of this made sense, since these fish seemed to me to be more like salmon than Montana trout. I tied up several dozen giant black Wooly Buggers and Zonkers that I felt would be large enough to entice a 30-pound brown trout, and many probably resembled a baby seal or whatever they ate at sea. I'd seen some pretty impressive brown trout mouths in Montana, so it was hard to imagine the mouth on a 30-pound male that spent its life in the ocean.

"Big flies, big fish" made a lot of sense, so I left my extensive collection of nymphs and small Wooly Buggers at home. Big mistake! The lesson here is when you are going to a new place for a new fish, do not leave anything at home.

Fortunately, the lodge manager graciously picked up a dozen flies from the local shop for me, all of which resembled the hundreds of normal trout nymphs I had left at home. Tierra del Fuego trout are, in fact, still trout. The biggest fish caught all week fell to size 12 nymphs. One of the biggest concerns in this fishing was straightening out the size 10 and 12 hooks with our 10- and 12-pound-test leaders. As it turned out, giant black Wooly Buggers and Zonkers work best during high water, so your fly selection is really controlled by water conditions rather than feeding patterns.

The Rio Grande was a joy to wade, and usually one side was considerably deeper than the other. It was a simple process to wade out until your best cast would just reach the far bank. The program was to cast across the river, let your line sink the fly, and then swing it across. Most of the strikes came at the start of the swing, and there was no way of telling how many you missed on the dead drift. I found it helpful to retrieve very, very slowly during the drifting phase, just enough to keep the line tight. If you were not snagging bottom every other cast, you weren't deep enough. Solution: Change to the next level line. As I mentioned, every pool was a new combination of current, depth, and wind.

My second trip to Tierra del Fuego, however, was a bit frustrating. With the river several feet higher and many knots faster than the year before, wading was tough. The soft pebble bottom that was so comforting at low water presented a stability problem in the strong current. You couldn't wade as close to the far bank, and there was all that fast water between you and the fish. The spey casters really had an advantage in those conditions, and I really needed a 10-weight and a heavy sinking line. The Teeny 300 was swept away like straw. Unfortunately, you have to book the better lodges a year in advance, so you really must check on the river condition just before you leave on your trip.

This brown was 37 inches, but one measuring 36 inches was 4 pounds heavier.

Chico Fernández with a nice brown and a spey rod.
CHICO FERNÁNDEZ

In the net. CHICO FERNÁNDEZ

We routinely fished till dark, and the sunsets were spectacular.
CHICO FERNÁNDEZ

Tierra del Fuego is famous for its wind, but most times you will be casting with the wind at your back, which can actually be an advantage. If it is off the wrong shoulder, simply turn around and drop your backcast like we do tarpon fishing. I had been told repeatedly that a week in Tierra del Fuego would give me a new definition of "wind," but it really wasn't as bad as I expected, and it did not interfere with the fishing even when it hit 55 mph one afternoon. The bottom line was that the fish did not care. Putting a 20-pound brown trout in the air takes your mind off a lot of problems.

These are really big fish, and they jump like salmon. The strikes could be as subtle as a snag in the weeds or a jolt that could pop a 10-pound tippet. Once hooked, these fish spent half their time in the air! The runs were not stupendous, but occasionally one of the big ones would take off downstream heading for the ocean. Most hit a swinging nymph with no more force than a clump of weeds. Usually, the fly would simply stop, and an increase in pressure met no more reaction than a very subtle head shake—

In spite of the wind, the idea was to drift the fly along the far bank for as long as possible. CHICO FERNÁNDEZ

just enough to tell you it was a fish and a big one to boot. My two biggest browns measured 37 and 35 inches, and both had girths over 20 inches. The very last afternoon I jumped and lost four fish that I know were over 20 pounds, all on size 10 nymphs tied locally in Rio Grande. Ted Gabreski caught the biggest fish of our week, measuring 36½ by 25½, again on a size 12 nymph. That fish, by the way, computes to 30 pounds. Bob Stearns caught two browns that taped out over 25 pounds on bombers that made his entire trip a success. If the wind lays down, you really need to break out the floating line and work the surface. The strikes are spectacular!

Maria Behety covers the first 30 miles or so of fishable Rio Grande water, so the trout are fresh from the sea and silver. As they work upstream, like steelhead, they revert to their species' normal, more colorful state. We caught several browns in the upper pools that actually looked like brown trout. As the river meanders north into Chile, there are more bluffs, hills, and trees to block the wind. In the Chilean sections, the pools are more forgiving for the novice caster. The fish run from 8 to 20 pounds, which is somewhat smaller than what we experienced. There are quite a few quality lodges up and down the Rio Grande. Perhaps the main questions to ask your outfitter when planning a trip are (1) how far a drive is it to the water each day?; (2) what's the top weight fish we can realistically expect?; (3) how much will all this cost?—lodge prices can vary by several thousand dollars; and (4) when are the best water conditions? That last question is always a zinger! Arrangements to fish Tierra del Fuego can be made by contacting The Fly Shop at (800) 669-3474 or Frontiers at (800) 245-1950.

Twilight on the Rio Grande often produced the best dry-fly action. CHICO FERNÁNDEZ

Striped Marlin

PAT FORD

Puerto Aroya is the home base for most of the Galapagos tours.

The Galapagos Islands are undoubtedly the best place in the world to catch a world-class striped marlin on a fly—if you can find a way to fish there, and conditions are right. Like anywhere else, there are times when the bite just doesn't happen, and the fishing is pretty frustrating. But when the bite is on, it's not unusual to have shots at thirty to fifty striped marlin per day. The only problem, if any, is that the great majority of them will be in the 200-pound range—a size not particularly compatible with a fly rod. The other problem is that commercial sportfishing is restricted in the islands.

The Galapagos Islands are separated from the coast of Ecuador by some 600 miles of ocean. The archipelago is made up of fifteen large islands and a great number of small ones, each with something unique to offer. The most efficient way to tour this unique national park is on a live-aboard ship that will allow you to spend a day at each island, combining snorkeling with eco-land touring. It is a photographer's paradise, with multiple species of flowers and wildlife. In 1835, the British naturalist Charles Darwin visited the islands and formulated the "Evolution of Species." The Charles Darwin Museum is located on Santa Cruz in the town of Puerto Ayora, which is the starting point for most of the tourist operations. Commercial sportfishing, however, is just beginning in the islands and has been an on-again, off-again enterprise for the last several years.

It's not bragging if it's true. LUIS EDUARDO GOMEZ HIDALGO

Sportsfishing boats in San Crystobal for the 2005 Striped Marlin Tournament. LUIS EDUARDO GOMEZ HILDAGO

Almost all of the conventional fishing in done with lures.

Historically, commercial sportfishing had never been allowed in park waters, which is why it is so spectacular. After considerable politicking, Miamian Tim Choate teamed up with Braden Escobar and obtained permission to operate a 35-foot Bertram, *Striper*, out of Puerto Ayora with certain restrictions: No billfish were to be killed, lures could only have one hook, and only circle hooks could be used with live baits. Every effort possible was to be invoked to release all marlin unharmed. Eventually, Choate and Escobar parted ways. Braden continued the original operation and Tim was given permission to introduce a second charter boat. This time, he teamed up with Jaime Ortiz and brought another 35 Bertram, *Trueno*, over to the islands with Alan Starr as its captain. Alan retired from the coast guard after a dozen years and devoted the rest of his life to sportfishing from Massachusetts to the Florida Keys to Australia and most everywhere in between.

Stripes range from 125 pounds to over 300 . . .

. . . making fly fishing a real challenge.

Today, the limited sportfishing that is available in the Galapagos Islands is pretty much the result of the efforts of a small number of concerned anglers, such as IGFA reps Luis Eduardo Gomez, Pepe Anton, and Francisco "Paco" Sola.

Getting to the islands is actually not as difficult as you would expect. There are flights into Guayaquil, Ecuador, from most major cities, but it is necessary to spend a night in Guayaquil because the daily commercial flights to the Galapagos leave at 9 A.M. The Four Points Sheraton in Guayaquil is first class and only minutes from the airport. The flight to the islands takes about ninety minutes.

Galapagos's airport is located on Baltra, a small island separated from Santa Cruz by a channel that is easily crossed by ferry. A taxi then takes you over the mountains of Santa Cruz to the city of Puerto Ayora on the exact opposite side of the island. There are several acceptable hotels in Puerto Ayora and many interesting restaurants. One point to consider is that the Galapagos Islands are literally on the equator, and between December and May, it can be pretty hot. If you are not used to 100-degree temperatures, be sure you have a hotel with air-conditioning. Returning each evening to a room with only a ceiling fan can make sleeping pretty difficult.

Naturally the best jumps that I caught with the camera were of fish hooked on conventional tackle.

The striped marlin's first jump can easily cover 300 yards.

Everyone else managed to boat a stripe on fly except me—I'll just have to go back.

You should be settled into your room by noon, and after lunch, a trip can be arranged to the highlands to see the world famous Galapagos Tortoise in its natural habitat along with a series of interesting natural caves. The entire trip can be done in a few hours for a $25 cab fare. A trip to the Charles Darwin Museum is a "must see" but is actually much less interesting than the highland tour. The day after your arrival, the fishing starts!

Sea conditions in the Galapagos are calmest between December and June. From late June to December, a 3-foot to 5-foot chop is common, making conditions safe but sometimes a bit uncomfortable. The fish are still there, however, and October and November can be spectacular—but you do need a good pair of sea legs. The absolute best months to fish the Galapagos out of Santa Cruz according to Captain Starr are April and May—seas are calm and the striped marlin concentrate around various undersea mountains and banks in huge numbers. The moon phase doesn't seem to affect the bite in April and May, but Captain Starr feels that it does in January, Feb-

This fly-hooked striper has brilliant colors.

ruary, and March. In those months, five days before and five days after the new moon are the most productive. The week before and after the full moon can be pretty frustrating. On a good day on the new moon, the *Trueno* may raise forty marlin; on the full moon, you may raise four—a big difference.

Most of the fishing out of Puerto Ayora is done at an undersea plateau called "First National Bank." It is about an hour run from the port, and it's not unusual to see

Rufus Wakeman pulls on a small striped marlin that to my displeasure refused to jump.

Big fly, big reel, and a big rod are needed for striped marlin.

hoards of dolphin and sea lions working the surface. There are other areas, such as Gordon Rocks, a small island of mostly rock, that provide exceptional tuna and wahoo catches.

Probably 90 percent of the sport fishing in the Galapagos is done by trolling high-speed marlin lures. If you want to fly-fish, it's a simple matter to keep one outrigger up and troll two hookless lures and a big teaser. The technique is the same as for sailfish in Guatamala or Costa Rica—it's just that the Galapagos stripes are huge and mean. Fighting one of the these beauties on a fly rod is not for the weak of heart or back.

If the bite is off at First National Bank, there is an alternative. There is another area off the east coast of San Cristobal called White Rose Bank where the moon doesn't seem to affect the fishing in February and March. White Rose is a 70-mile run from Puerto Ayora, so you have to either go directly to San Cristobal or leave Santa Cruz in the morning for the 3 1/2-hour run to San Cristobal, fish all day, and then overnight in San Cristobal at the Casablanca Hotel or sleep in the boat until your return. If the bite is slow at one place, it is usually good at the other, so you have to be flexible and go where the fish are.

The first and only sportfishing tournament ever held in the Galapagos was in February 2005. Ten private boats raised 1,500 marlin and released 400 in three days—all based out of San Cristobal. However, Captain Starr has seen days when over seventy stripes were raised just a half

Rufus shows off his first striped marlin, a baby by Galapagos standards.

hour out of Puerto Ayora. The key for the angler is to be in touch with the outfitter and the boat captain to find out whether the fishing is going to be better in Santa Cruz or in San Cristobal and to make plans accordingly. If you wait until you arrive in the islands, it may be too late to get a hotel room in San Cristobal, which is not exactly Key West as far as accommodations go. Many times, it's best to simply sleep on the boat, if that is possible.

IGFA President Rob Kramer fished San Cristobal's White Rose Bank with IGFA Trustee Pepe Anton, Luis Gomez, and "Paco" Sola in February 2005. They actually slept on Pepe's boat, describing conditions in town as "pretty basic." I have been told that there are about as many sea lions walking around town as people. Rob found an amazing difference in water temperature between San Cristobal—69 degrees—and the currents on White Rose Bank, where the water temperature reached 80 degrees. His group fished only some thirteen hours over two days, but they had 302 strikes and released 101 marlin between 150 and 300 pounds. By the end of each day, no one wanted to even touch a rod, they were so tired.

You really need to be able to raise a lot of aggressive marlin to switch one of these brutes over to a fly, which is why the Galapagos Islands are the best place in the world to catch a striped marlin on a fly. Again, the choice of poppers versus streamers is pretty much a matter of personal preference, but in over thirty years of teasing billfish, I have found that the bite-to-hookup ratio greatly improves without the popper head. Simply casting the fly behind and to the right of the fish and letting it lay still

Marine iguanas are unique to the Galapagos Islands and willingly pose for the camera.

This covers most of the daily activity of blue-footed boobies— looking left and looking right.

Sally lightfoot crabs liven up the shorelines.

One way to scratch your back.

The vicious galapagos "tortuga gigante."

results in far more strikes than stripping the fly. Since none of the Galapagos striped marlin will be killed, there is no need to strictly adhere to IGFA rules unless you are an extreme purist. The idea is to have fun and jump some fish. Records are not possible, so why worry about technicalities—a 2- or 3-foot shock leader really helps keep these big boys on the line.

If there is a problem with the striped marlin of the Galapagos, it's the size—the great majority of the fish will be over 200 pounds and can range up to 400 pounds. The 100-pounders are the most fun on a fly but are fairly rare, so my recommendation is to "supersize" your fly tackle. The rod should be at least a 15-weight and probably heavier. I prefer my big game rods to look a little more like a fly rod than a push pole, but not much. My favorite is the Lamiglas Blue Water Series 15-weight and Biscayne Rods 18-weight. And even with these monster rods, at times I have prayed for a little more lifting power. You need a reel comparable to the Tibor Pacific or the Abel 5 filled with at least 500 yards of 50-pound (synthetic) backing. I add 100 yards of 50-pound or 60-pound bright yellow dacron line on top of the backing and then 50 yards of 50-pound fluorescent mono to provide some stretch. My fly line is always a 700- or 800-grain shooting taper or Jim Teeny's Billy Pate billfish line. The leader-tippet combination doesn't need to be much more than 8 feet long, and fly selection is a matter of personal preference—if the fish is teased properly, it will strike most any color fly. Again, a double hook rig with 6/0 octopus-style hooks behind a tube fly provides the most hookups. No matter how experienced you are, a 200-pound striped marlin on a fly is an adrenaline rush beyond compare.

No matter how many days you fish, be sure to have a day or two at the end for some eco-touring. We rented a glass bottom one day for $135 that took us all round Santa Cruz to visit Tortuga Bay and shorelines with marine iguanas, sea lions, and blue-footed boobies—a sort of seagull on steroids with powder blue feet. The Galapagos Islands really are a wonderland of natural beauty.

For more information about fishing for striped marlin in the Galapagos Islands, contact Tim Choate at Artmarina .com or Braden Escobar at Fishgalapagos.com.

Tigerfish

PAT FORD

You fish behind a wide variety of structure on the Lower Zambezi.

Captain Issack shows off a 16-pound tiger.

I have tried to hunt down and catch just about every remotely accessible fish that might be persuaded to eat a fly, and my favorite of all time is the tigerfish in the Zambezi River in Africa. I first laid eyes on a tigerfish on Larry Dahlberg's *The Hunt for Big Fish* on ESPN. Then one day I ran into Lance Glaser, who accompanied Larry on many of his trips, and I only had one question: "Of all the places you and Larry have fished, which was the most fun?" Without a second's hesitation, Lance said "Chiawa Camp in the Lower Zambezi National Park." He described a safari camp that had several fishing boats on the Lower Zambezi River and then showed me photos of a creature with fangs rather than teeth that looked like a mutant striped bass. They were like nothing I had ever seen. He explained that the tigerfish season is pretty much limited to about six weeks starting in late September, which is the peak of the dry season. After the first week of November, the rains begin, and the whole area soon becomes pretty much uninhabitable. But during October, the water is low, and the tigerfish are spawning and ready to attack most anything they see.

It didn't take long to convince me that catching a tigerfish would be a good excuse to visit Africa. Unfortunately,

This is the essence of Chiawa Camp. GRANT CUMINGS

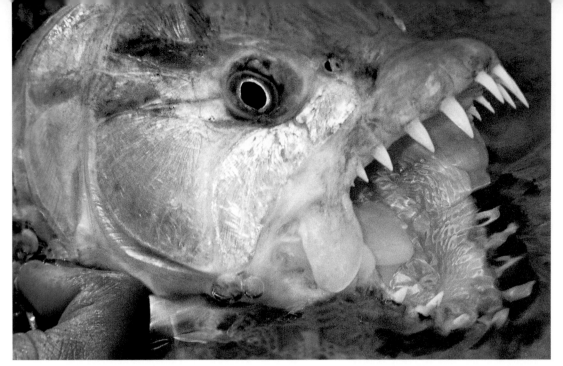

A tigerfish dental array is quite impressive.

the only person I knew who had even seen one was Larry Dahlberg. Larry had been to Chiawa Camp several times prior to my visit and still goes there most every year. These days, Larry's travel arrangements are made by Steve Yatomi at Adventure Travel Alliance, and they just can't seem to get enough of Chiawa Camp. Larry was a big help, and as it turned out, was actually at the camp when we arrived.

Our trip began with a flight from Miami to Atlanta and then to Johannesburg in South Africa. The flight is long, but overnight, so you can spend most of it asleep if you are lucky. From Johannesburg, we flew to Lusaka, Zambia, where we were met by lodge owners Dave and Jenny Cummings. The next phase was a small charter plane and a thirty-minute flight to the Jeki Airstrip in the Lower Zambezi National Park. Grant Cummings runs the camp, and he or one of his guides meets all the guests at the plane in one of the camp's Land Rovers. When the plane lands, get out your cameras—you are officially on safari. The ride to the camp is spectacular. We saw elephants, Cape buffalo by the hundreds, zebras, baboons, warthogs, lions, impalas, and dozens of other creatures before we even unpacked our luggage. On this trip, a good camera or video camera is just as important as your fishing gear.

Tigerfish don't get over 20 pounds very often, and while the Lower Zambezi River is about 2 miles wide, small islands and sandbars are everywhere, so fishing is relatively easy. Tigerfish are predators—the ultimate predator in the river. They actually do look a lot like a striped bass, average about the size of a big bonefish, and have a mouth that should have been designed in a sci-fi horror film. I am told that there is some form of slime on their razor-sharp fangs that is an anticoagulant, so if you are accidently bit-

Even the little guys are great fun. GRANT CUMINGS

A big tiger will suck in a fly with ease.

Nine- and 10-weight fly rods with full sinking lines are perfect for tigerfish in the Lower Zambezi.

Bright-colored, flashy synthetic flies work best and hold up to tigerfish teeth.

ten, you will bleed for the next week. The tigerfish's attack pattern consists of a quick strike to cripple its prey and then a relaxed return for the kill. Many times I failed to get a hookup on that first hit and just let the fly hang in the current for the second attack. Once hooked, the tigerfish hits the air, rattling its gills like a tarpon, and in short spurts, it has the speed of a bonefish. The fight is spectacular but usually relatively short compared to saltwater fish. Over the years, I have noticed that the top of the freshwater line—tigerfish, peacock bass, and golden dorado—all fight savagely, but have nowhere near the stamina of a permit or bonefish. Nevertheless, the first few minutes are pretty intense, to say the least.

I found that the heavy side of conventional bass tackle was plenty for tigerfish, with pixie spoons, size 6 Vibrex spinners, and swimming plugs like Rappalas being the most productive, but I was really interested in fly fishing. The information Larry Dahlberg gave to me turned out to be right on the money, so I am passing it on. A 10-weight rod is perfect for casting long distances with relatively big flies, and big flies help you catch big fish. A 9-weight makes casting too much work, and an 11-weight rod is simply too heavy. Tigerfish are not surface feeders, so you need a sinking line. The Teeny type 300- and 400-grain lines worked, but not as well as the full sinking number IV striper line. With the full sinking line, you do not need lead eyes on the flies, which makes casting a lot more pleasant. Depending on the stiffness of the rod, I sometimes use an 11-weight line on the 10-weight rod, but that is a personal preference. Whatever rod-and-line combo you decide on should be the one you can cast the farthest with the least effort. Leaders were easy and short—4 feet was plenty, but you do need a trace of light wire, 30-pound test or less, if you want the fish to stay attached for more than a few seconds. Lots of different flies worked. I did very well with flashy, peacock

Most of the time, you don't know whether to fish or take pictures.

bass–style flies, yet others did fine with plain white deceiver patterns. Larry is a big fan of the deer hair diver (naturally), but in truth, they all catch fish—if you put them in the right place, which is a few feet off the bottom.

The Zambezi River is like nothing you have ever seen. There are hard sandbars everywhere, usually full of hippos. A park survey found 75 hippos and 150 crocodiles per kilometer, so wading is not very popular. I mentioned early on to Grant that it would be very effective to wade the edge of the sandbars, working the dropoffs and cuts. Grant agreed it would be effective, but figured you'd make about 50 yards tops before a

This is my 14-pound, 8-ounce IGFA-record tigerfish from 1999.

On land, hippos are faster than you expect and very dangerous.

Mala Mala takes great pride in how well the animals tolerate the Land Rovers.

croc grabbed you. They take their animals very seriously in Africa, and we took him at his word—nobody got out of the boat!

The islands and bars form cuts, holes, and currents, each of which will hold at least one big tigerfish. In the beginning, the guide would motor right up into the hole and shut down. Eventually, we convinced him that it would be better to shut down outside the area and sneak up on it, and almost every time we came in quietly, one of the first few casts produced a double-digit fish. The wider areas were simply drifted and dredged. If there was a current mix that produced small tigers, the bigger ones were usually behind them in the deeper water. Basically, the fish were everywhere. My advice on landing them—let the guide grab the them. We didn't have any problems, but I have heard that crocs get excited by all the commotion and often grab fish right next to the boat—so keep your hands out of the water. A Boga Grip is very handy to have and makes it easier and safer to handle the fish for photos and releases.

Chiawa Camp's guides know the river well and would hold the boat below each fishing area for about ten minutes before moving up the current and starting the drift. They eventually explained that the reason for this strain on our patience was to spot hippos who stay submerged, walking around the bottom, for up to six minutes or so. The hippo families are usually near the shore or on a sandbar and easy to spot, but the bulls are solitary, walking along the bottom with only their ears, eyes, and nose, if that, out of the water. A boat floating into a bull hippo's "territory" could attract a lot of unpleasant attention, so it was wise to spot the creatures before you started fishing so you could give them a wide berth.

Even with care, hippos were popping up a hundred feet away every now and then with a "whoosh" similar to a whale breaking water. These are very large and unpleas-

The smaller male tigers are very aggressive. Their relatively small mouths don't stop them from attacking prey half their size.

ant creatures, but they sure make the fishing exciting. You are almost always within sight of a few hippos, not to mention the crocs on the shore and the Cape buffalo and elephants on the islands. To say that this is an adventurous river is an understatement. I think I spent as much time with a camera in my hand as I did with a fishing rod.

Chiawa Camp, by the way, has an unblemished safety record and takes great pride in the fact that their guests don't even get sick, much less hurt. Guests are given comprehensive briefings upon arrival, and all activities are led by qualified and experienced guides with first-aid training. Each cabin has a personal two-way radio for emergencies that is scanned 24/7 by camp management. Chiawa Camp has 24-hour contact with the rest of the world by both computer and satellite phone. They don't leave anything to chance.

Chiawa Camp has been owned and operated by the Cummings family since it opened in 1989. It was the first safari camp to be established in the Lower Zambezi National Park and remains the only camp in the park that is still owned by its founders.

The daily routine at Chiawa Camp is simple. Wake early to coffee and cookies in your cabin, fish from 7 A.M. to 10 A.M., and then return to camp for an enormous breakfast. After breakfast, we would fish until lunch around 2 P.M., after which we would either go back out fishing until dark or go on a game drive in the Land Rovers. Even if we fished until sundown, we would still go out on a night drive for a few hours before dinner. During our visit to Chiawa Camp, it was hot during the day but dry, and as soon as the sun went down, it cooled off nicely for comfortable sleeping. The bugs weren't a problem, and the food was outstanding. It was the complete package. Every horror story I had heard about visiting Africa didn't apply to this trip. You could drink the water and eat the salads and fruit without fear, which was a very pleasant surprise. The Cummings have even upgraded the boats since my trip to larger, safer 18-foot pontoon boats that are easy to fish from. Cameras are a must, and you should bring at least a 400mm lens to take full advantage of the wildlife. I prefer the digital Cannon D20 with the 100 to 400mm zoom lens.

I really can't say enough about Chiawa Camp's program or how much fun the tigerfish are to catch. The only possible glitch in this otherwise amazing vacation is that the Lower Zambezi National Park does not have any cheetahs or rhinos to look at, and as long as you're in Africa, you might as well see and photograph as much wildlife as possible. Grant Cummings solved the problem with the

This ten-year-old is the dominant male in the Mala Mala Reserve.

A Mala Mala leopard with an impala kill.

Lodge owner and manager Grant Cummings really will give you the trip of a lifetime. STEVE YATOMI

suggestion that we follow our week at Chiawa Camp with a few days at the Mala Mala Game Reserve in South Africa, which was literally on the way home. When we left Chiawa, we returned to Johannesburg, but instead of flying home, we took another plane to the Kruger Airport, where we were met and driven to the Mala Mala Main Camp and twenty-five air-conditioned rooms overlooking the Sand River.

The Mala Mala Game Reserve covers 33,000 acres that years ago successfully converted from hunting to photographic safaris. The vast array of habitat is the key factor in the incredible amount of wildlife and the complexity of its fauna and flora. At Mala Mala, you can plan on viewing Africa's "Big 5" almost every day. It is said that Mala Mala is the best game-viewing destination in the world, and I can't argue. The game-drive program is basically the same as Chiawa Camp's, but the animal life is incredible. It is the perfect complement to the Chiawa tigerfish experience and highly recommended for everyone—especially the photographers. If you love to fish, this is definitely the way to see Africa.

To book a week with Grant and his friends, call Steve Yatomi's Adventure Travel Alliance at (800) 254-Fish and check out the camp's Web site at Chiawa.com.

To arrange a few days in Mala Mala, check out Mala Mala.com and Go2Africa.com. They can set up your visit and flights to suit your specific needs and timetable.

Reflections on Some Good Days

Captain Rick Murphy lets his skiff glide to the edge of the flat 20 yards south of Christian Point, just a mile or so from Flamingo in Florida Bay. It's dawn, and the only sounds are the squawking of marsh birds and the splashes of small tarpon as they make a meal out of some unknown prey floating with the tide. The sun is just starting to spread a golden hue over the horizon.

A short cast sends my synthetic furball of a fly to a small pocket in the mangroves. I don't move the fly 2 feet before a baby tarpon eats it and starts its show, making gyrating, gill-rattling, back-flipping leaps, just like its big brothers do. It's mid-September, the quiet time in south Florida. The summer has not yet ended; it's still hot and humid. But it's one of the best times of the year to be in Florida Bay. There are no crowds, and plenty of redfish, snook, and small tarpon just waiting to hit a nicely placed fly. These are no-pressure fish—the fun kind.

As Rick releases the day's first tarpon, it occurs to me that a long time ago I had a major misconception about fly fishing: I thought the sport had something to do with *catching*. I was heavy into tournaments then. I was itching to catch the biggest fish on the lightest tippet to win the admiration and envy of my peers.

As a member of the Miami Beach Rod and Reel Club, I fished for every species imaginable with fly tackle just to get points awarded by the club. I even tallied some pretty respectable fish. I landed a bunch of permit on flies during the 1970s by adding a split shot to the hook so the fly would drop to the bottom when you stopped retrieving it. Now you can use lead eyeballs that look a lot spiffier but accomplish the same thing—make the fly dive for the grass like a crab, a permit's natural prey, does.

I spent three years trying to catch a sailfish on a fly off Florida's east coast, and finally did it in January 1980—a 55½-pound prize that is still the Florida state fly-rod record twenty-five years later. A 73-pound white marlin and 67½-pound cobia that I caught on 8-pound-test tippets were still International Game Fish Association records two decades later. Actually, the cobia is the only fish on the IGFA's books where the fly-rod record was larger than the general line class record. But today I look back and can hardly believe I killed

145

all those fish in the name of sport. I suppose I wasn't really any different than anyone else. Back then, we thought the supply of fish would go on forever.

My introduction to saltwater fly fishing began when the Navy sent me to Key West some thirty-five years ago. Not long after arriving in the Keys, I met a young writer named Thomas McGuane, who even then was an avid fly fisherman. Regrettably, I didn't get to know Tom very well, but he was the first person to show me how to rig a fly rod for tarpon.

I remember that he was building his first flats boat, a sleek gray-and-white Fibercraft, and that he didn't want to catch anything that lived in more than 3 feet of water. All he did was fly-fish. He never brought a fish to the dock, and he never weighed anything. He just wanted to absorb the sensation of a tarpon, bonefish, or, occasionally, a permit inhaling his fly and unleashing its raw power at the sting of the hook. He never seemed to care if he "officially" landed the fish; he just wanted to give it a good run for its money and then say thanks for the experience. Tom McGuane was way ahead of his time.

It was probably fifteen years ago that I realized I didn't care if I ever caught another fish on a spinning rod. I remember the day very well. It was one of my first trips with Rick Murphy. We were in Florida Bay. It was September. There was no wind, and birds were everywhere—pelicans, ibises, ospreys, spoonbills, herons, flamingos, you name it. Some flew by in V-shaped flocks, others were perched in the mangrove branches, and some waded the shoreline and flats searching for food. Everywhere you looked, something was happening.

We were in Rick's jon boat—a 16-foot aluminum skiff powered by a 30-horsepower Yamaha motor. It had no poling platform, no casting deck, no bait well or fish box, just a couple of coolers and some fly rods. It went pretty fast over a slick surface. It didn't seem to matter if there was any water under it at all: It ran just as well through mud and grass, and that was the idea. That jon boat could reach places a $30,000 flats boat never could.

As we streaked across Snake Bight that morning, we could see wakes dart out ahead of us as a sheepshead or catfish panicked at our sudden intrusion into its otherwise tranquil world. The sun hadn't yet appeared over the horizon, and in many directions it was impossible to tell where sea left off and sky began. The clouds were just as distinct on the water's surface as they were in the sky. Life does not get any more peaceful.

Every so often, Rick would stop the boat and take out his binoculars. Then we'd be off again. Finally, we shut down for good near a small channel that followed the mangrove shoreline. When the indignant squawking of the feathered residents subsided, the stillness returned. The splash of a baitfish was as noticeable as someone falling out of the boat.

Rick poled slowly toward a point where he knew currents met and where snook and tarpon lay in wait for baitfish. I could see the ripples of rolling tarpon, and a splash as one nailed a shrimp floating on the surface. These were not big fish—the "real" tarpon season was long since over. The 100-pounders had gone wherever it is they go when they exit the Keys in mid-July. These were baby tarpon, mostly 5- to 20-pounders. Perfect for an 8- or 9-weight fly rod. Which is why we were there. As an aside, I actually prefer a 9-weight, because it doesn't really overpower the fish and makes casting bushy flies easier if the wind picks up.

Due to some unexplainable genetic imprinting, these tarpon like to hit small fluorescent poppers that don't resemble anything in nature. My old friend, Captain Bill Curtis, introduced me to the popper trick. Rick Murphy had been using them for years himself. It didn't matter what tippet we had on. This was fun fishing. No rules.

My first cast put the white-and-yellow popper a few feet out from the mangroves. I let it settle, put the rod tip in the water, and gave the line three short jerks. Bam! Two feet of tarpon nailed the popper and started hopping all over the place, as good tarpon do. He stayed in the channel, not dumb enough to run onto the flat where there was more mud and weed than water, or smart enough to head for the mangrove roots. After a few minutes, this gorgeous silver-plated creature lay next to the boat. Rick reached down, grabbed the popper, easily removed the barbless hook from the tarpon's nose, and off it went.

I aimed my next cast toward several rolling fish, moved the popper about 3 feet, and it was attacked. I set the hook as best you can on a tarpon, but it didn't stick; on the fish's fourth jump, the popper flew back at me.

As I tried to organize the line that was at that point pretty much draped all over me, a second tarpon nailed the popper. There was no hope of setting the hook, so this little guy disappeared after the first jump. I managed to get the line back in my hand and was just about to pick up for another cast when Rick said, "Pop it." I did, and tarpon number three was in the air. I've never had so much fun on one cast.

For two hours, the tarpon streamed by. I must have jumped forty fish. Almost all of them spit the hook after a few jumps, probably because I never really tried to set it very hard. One 40-pounder rolled by, but he wasn't interested. (The bigger tarpon, those over 20 pounds, don't seem to like poppers.) Finally, the antics of a nearby alligator and the heat of the day sent the tarpon into shaded waters deep in the mangroves. My poppers were chewed to bits by then anyway, so Rick fired up the motor and off we went across the flats.

We next found a big school of reds. I spotted two, but Rick saw something like thirty. As he poled us closer, I realized he was right—there were lots of fish around, but only after about forty casts and a lot of poling did we find a few fish dumb enough to eat. By the time we released the fourth fish, we figured that the others would be too spooky to be of much use. We ran around a bit and inspected a few keys where Rick found more tarpon, lots of sharks, and occasionally a snook, only one of which was overly interested in my fly, and it was really tiny.

There was one more area Rick wanted to hit on the falling tide, so we raced back through Snake Bight toward the channel that runs up to the northern shoreline of Flamingo. We could see a number of skiffs in the distant channel, stuck there because of the low water. Rick's jon boat was the only boat that could reach the fish that were now tailing on the flat.

As we got farther into the bight, the water was as slick as glass. Anything that moved left a wake. The reds were feeding, and every so often a spotted tail would flop above the surface. The water barely covered the weeds, so it was pretty hard to spot a fish if it didn't create some sort of disturbance.

Rick poled us from one tail to the next for about an hour, but nothing would eat—and I'd been casting so much that I was actually getting pretty accurate.

Once in a while, a red would spot the fly, charge over to it, and then stop. Changing patterns didn't help; the fish were just acting weird. Rick didn't even blame my casting, which also was unusual.

We were about to give up then Rick spotted two impressive wakes moving toward us. I managed a long cast and put the fly a few feet in front of where I figured the fish would be, which is usually a few feet in front of the actual wake. (Never cast right at the wake; you'll be behind the fish.)

The fly settled lightly in the extremely shallow water, and the lead fish attacked it. I set the hook by pure reflex, since I was so used to my offerings being ignored, and a big snook stuck its head out of the water and thrashed at the surface. This fish had some shoulders, and it raced around throwing mud and weeds in all directions.

When I finally got the snook to the boat, there was probably as much grass around the fly as there was fish. Rick calmly picked through the glop till he found the snook, then held it up. It was the biggest snook I'd ever caught on any type of tackle, and snook make delicious table fare, but there wasn't a doubt in my mind. "Let him go," I said. After a few photos and a little CPR, Rick and I watched the snook slowly swim away through the shallow water. Our day was over.

On the ride back that hot afternoon, I realized that something special had happened. I'd jumped a ton of tarpon that weren't big enough to get the fly line off the reel; I'd been outsmarted by dozens of redfish (which are closer in intelligence to alligators than bonefish); and I'd caught the largest and smallest snook of my angling career. Nothing had been measured, much less weighed; no club cards were filled out—why was it so much fun? The answer was obvious.

It's years later now as Rick poles us along Christian Point. Eric Herstedt and his charter come in behind us. They jump a tarpon, then another, and another. When Bill Curtis pulls up behind Eric, we decide to leave the point to them. Rick poles us out of the deeper water so he can get his customized tunnel drive Maverick on plane without spooking any fish.

In minutes, we're racing down a poorly marked channel toward Rankin Key to search for redfish. I know it's going to be a good day as I conjure up those few brief conversations I had about the essence of fly fishing in Key West over a quarter-century before. As we speed along, I hope that somewhere in Montana, an older, calmer, and wiser Thomas McGuane is having a good day, too. He taught me a lot. It just took a while for me to figure it out.